PSYCH

Most people are taught that the only reality is what we perceive through the five senses. But time and discovery often prove that our capability exceeds our imagination. How else can we explain the growing use of psychic ability in archaeology and criminal investigations—*in the 1990s.*

Now you can capitalize on your innate psychic power *without fear* when you uncover psychometry as a completely natural and useful human attribute! *How to Develop and Use Psychometry* provides all of the techniques and practices necessary to enhance this inherent human sense for psychic perception. This groundbreaking guide will teach you how to access and stimulate your natural latent talents through a variety of effective methods.

Discover the beneficial effects of honing the intuitive sense as you exercise your new talent over and over again! You'll be surprised to find your psychic ability so close at hand!

About the Author

Ted Andrews is a full-time author, student and teacher in the metaphysical and spiritual fields. He conducts seminars, symposiums, and workshops and lectures throughout the country on many facets of ancient mysticism. Ted works with past-life analysis, auric interpretation, numerology, the Tarot and the Qabala as methods of developing and enhancing inner potential. He is a clairvoyant and certified in spiritual mediumship, basic hypnosis, and acupressure. Ted is also involved in the study and use of herbs as an alternative path. In addition to writing several books, he is a contributing author to various metaphysical magazines.

To Write to the Author

If you wish to contact the author or would like more information about this book, please write to the author in care of Llewellyn Worldwide, and we will forward your request. Both the author and publisher appreciate hearing from you and learning of your enjoyment of this book and how it has helped you. Llewellyn Worldwide cannot guarantee that every letter written to the author can be answered, but all will be forwarded. Please write to:

Ted Andrews
c/o Llewellyn Worldwide
P.O. Box 64383-025, St. Paul, MN 55164-0383,
U.S.A.

Please enclose a self-addressed, stamped envelope for reply, or $1.00 to cover costs. If outside the U.S.A., enclose international postal reply coupon.

How to Develop and Use Psychometry

Ted Andrews

1995
Llewellyn Publications
St. Paul, Minnesota, 55164-0383

FIRST EDITION
Second Printing 1995

Cover Design by Lynne Menturweck
Book design by Laura Gudbaur

Cataloging-in-Publication Data
Andrews, Ted. 1952-
   How to develop and use psychometry/
   Ted Andrews
     p.   cm — (Llewellyn's how to series)
   Includes bibliographical references.
   ISBN 1-56718-025-6
   1. Psychology (Parapsychology) I. Title. II Series
BF1286.A53 1994   94-3524
133.8—dc20   CIP

Llewellyn Publications
A Division of Llewellyn Worldwide, Ltd.
P.O. Box 64383, St. Paul, Minnesota, 55164-0383

HOW TO DO IT!

No matter what it is, the important question always is: "How to do it?"

The mind has many marvelous powers—far more than you have ever dreamed of—and humanity has barely begun the wonderful evolutionary journey that will let us tap into them all at will. We grow in our abilities as we do things.

There are many wonderful things you can do. As you do them, you learn more about the innate qualities of mind and spirit, and as you exercise these inner abilities, they will grow in strength—as will your vision of your mental and spiritual potential.

In learning to *Develop and Use Psychometry*, or making a *Love Charm* or using a *Magic Mirror*, or many other strange and wonderful things, you are extending—just a little bit—the tremendous gift that lies within, the Life Force itself.

We are born that we may grow, and not to use this gift—not to grow in your perception and understanding of it—is to turn away from the gifts of Life, of Love, of Beauty, of Happiness that are the very reason for Creation.

Learning how to do these things is to open psychic windows to New Worlds of Mind & Spirit. Actually doing these things is to enter New Worlds. Each of these things that we do is a step forward in accepting responsibility for the worlds that you can shape and influence.

Simple, easy to follow, yet so very rewarding. Following these step-by-step instructions can start you upon high adventure. Gain control over the world around you, and step into *New Worlds of Mind & Spirit*.

To Jennifer & Arlinda (M.I.D.'s)

ACKNOWLEDGMENTS

So often we are touched by people and events in subtle but very catalytic ways. Every event and person that touches our life has the potential to impact upon it and add to the color and wonder of our experiences.

I wish to thank everyone at Llewellyn for their supportive touches in all my writing endeavors, particularly Carl and Sandra Weschcke, along with Nancy Mostad, who have made me feel such an integral part of the Llewellyn family.

Also I wish to thank the wonderful British medium, Bill Landis, whose "Flower Clairsentience" demonstrations continue to inspire my imagination and my own efforts toward yet further development of my abilities.

And I am ever grateful to Dr. Peter Moscow who by touching my life awakened new levels of friendship, respect and professionalism for me in the metaphysical community.

I wish also to express my gratitude for everyone I have touched in this field and whose support has touched me in ways that I may not have ever acknowledged individually. To all I am very thankful, and I hold you in my thoughts and prayers daily.

Other books by Ted Andrews

Simplified Magic
Imagick
The Sacred Power in Your Name
How to See & Read the Aura
The Magical Name
Dream Alchemy
Sacred Sounds
How to Meet and Work with Spirit Guides
How to Uncover Your Past Lives
Magickal Dance
Enchantment of the Faerie Realm
The Occult Christ
Animal-Speak
Sacred Sound
The Healer's Manual

Forthcoming

Crystal Balls and Crystal Bowls
How to Develop Psychic Powers

Contents

Contents

❧ 1 ❧
Seeing Through Touch

Imagine that you have gone to visit an old friend, someone you have not seen in years. You are invited in and told to make yourself comfortable while he or she moves off to another room to change clothes, or to ready some snacks for your visit.

You settle yourself comfortably in the nearest chair. Immediately, you know that this is your friend's favorite. It is a little more worn than the other furniture, but it is not its appearance that tells you this is the favorite. There is something more—something indefinable.

You relax, settling into the chair. As you sit there, you begin to realize that much has changed since you last saw your friend. So far, you have only had a few moment's contact, but you have noticed so much.

You realize there is a great amount of nervousness about your visit. You can feel your friend's tension in your own body, as if it is being passed directly to you from the chair itself. You wonder if there are money problems, but brush that impression aside when you look at the decor of your friend's home. This is not the home of someone struggling financially.

You begin to feel sad and alone. For some reason, your friend's mother comes to mind. You wonder how she is doing, if her health is all right. It has been so long since you have had any contact, you hope that everything is fine with her as well. The more you focus on her, the more nervous you find yourself getting.

Then, you are no longer comfortable sitting in that chair. You feel a strong need to move. You have all this nervous energy suddenly and no where to put it. You stand, breaking contact with the chair, and begin to feel better. You breathe more deeply. Although you are no longer feeling the tension, you still remember it, and move about the room distracting yourself by looking over titles in the bookcase, or viewing a wall painting more closely. You occupy your mind and distract yourself from what you had been feeling in the chair.

As you relax, you smile at yourself. How silly of you! You must be more nervous about seeing your old friend than you realized. You rationalize your feelings as originating from your own nerves. Any impressions about your friend's current state probably was nothing more than being able to read your friend's voice and body language. After all, you were once very close. While growing up, you went everywhere together. Didn't your parents often joke about the two of you sharing the same brain? You chuckle softly to yourself in memory of it, and the last tension slips away, as your friend returns and greets you a second time.

As the visit continues, you catch up on each other's lives. You find your friend, like you, really was nervous about your visit. Things have been hectic at work; there has been much overtime and little playtime. Your friend's mother has been ill, and expenses for care have increased to the point to where it is becoming difficult to cover them.

Although most of what you felt while sitting in your friend's chair is confirmed, the intensity of that experience is lost or softened. It has settled to a vague sense of "I knew something wasn't right," but you no longer even realize when that feeling came upon you—much less how it did.

We often have experiences such as this, but, unfortunately, we have learned to deny them. We shut them down or ignore them. To a great degree, we have been socialized away from honoring our more subtle insights and responses. After all, the psychic realm is just the stuff of fiction or simply a product of the imagination. At best, it is one of those unusual and unexplainable circumstances that we will take out and dust off periodically to add spice to otherwise colorless conversations and dull social occasions.

We have all had experiences where we felt something or knew something, but we rationalized it, brushed it aside or even suppressed it entirely. We refused to acknowledge it, because we are taught that only what we experience through the five senses is real. We attribute it to something in the person's voice, the body language or any outside clue that we can attribute to one of the five senses.

Even today, with all of the evidence available, many believe that anything of the psychic realm is not for the mainstream. It is only suitable for the "oddball," but almost everyone in the mainstream has had impressions such as in the scenario described above.

What if a chair could speak? What stories would your furniture tell if it could only talk? What if you could pick up a person's pen and tell exactly what kind of day he or she had? What new insights to history could we gain from objects of antiquity if they could speak? What if you could touch someone and be able to sense where there was illness or aches and pains? What if you could hold a picture or favorite toy of a lost child and be able to see what has happened?

The human being has a sensitivity that goes far beyond what is often defined for us, and beyond what we often imagine. In this book, we will examine the reality reflected in the questions above. With a little awareness and practice, you will learn to develop your natural senses to read through touch what has imprinted itself on objects, people, and places. You will discover that you are naturally psychic and sensitive to all you touch, and all that touches you.

Clairsentience and Psychometry

Everyone is psychic. If you have ever had any psychic experience, you can have it again, and again, and again. If you have ever had insight or information on a person or events with whom you are not familiar, you are psychic.

Psychic impressions come in a variety of forms. It may simply be a hunch, a vague sense of something impending, or even a flash of sudden insight. It may come as an auditory signal, as if someone is speaking to you outside of you, or even in your own head. It may come through a vision or a dream. You may catch a fragrance out of the blue that reminds you of something important. It may come as a passing thought.

Some even experience tastes that provide insight into resolving issues or events about to unfold. It is not unusual for me to experience tastes when I am doing healing work with clients.

It helps me to define problem areas. For example, if I start tasting caffeine while working on someone, it very likely indicates too much caffeine in his or her system. I might recommend cutting back on coffee, chocolate, or pop, since these are the three biggest sources of caffeine in our society. It may also indicate a need for increased water intake by the individual. The water helps to further dilute and break down the caffeine in the body so that it can eliminate it more easily.

Most people believe we have only five senses. I like to think of the human being as comprised of seven: sight, sound, touch, taste, smell, common sense, intuitive sense.

The true sixth sense, common sense, is the heightening and integration of what we experience with the traditional five senses. Understanding and using them to their fullest capacity is part of this. When we are able to integrate and understand what they are saying to us, we can open up to awareness beyond what the physical senses can tell us. Common sense helps us to see the patterns of our life as defined by the physical senses. The intuitive sense then helps us recognize where those patterns are likely to lead.

We can learn to use the physical senses to provide information that will help us to see the effects of that information on any level. For example, any good psychic is one who is able to see connections. If you can assess what has brought an individual to where he or she is are now, it is fairly easy to determine where that will lead. This is particularly true since most people never change their patterns, even when they recognize them. When we learn to heighten and integrate what we experience through the five senses through application of common sense, then the intuitive sense begins to awaken.

The key to utilizing the intuitive sense is the subconscious mind. All psychic impressions, as with most of the body's energies, are mediated by the subconscious mind. It is aware of everything that we encounter and express on the subtlest of levels. Because we rarely work with the subconscious mind, or believe we can control it, we often remain ignorant of what it perceives.

We don't have to remain in the dark, though. There are a variety of ways to access the subconscious mind. For those impressions to be recognized, they must be translated to the conscious mind. Meditation and hypnosis are two of the most obvious ways of doing this. They teach us how to shift the conscious mind to deeper, more subconscious levels.

Regardless of the means of accessing the subconscious mind's perceptions, they still will most often be translated through the five physical senses. This is because most psychic impressions are often extensions of the five physical senses.

These intuitive levels of experience and perception of the subconscious mind correlate strongly with the physical senses:

- Physical sight extends to become clairvoyance.
- Physical hearing extends to become clairaudience.
- Physical touch extends to become clairsentience.
- Physical smell extends to become clairaroma.[1]
- Physical taste extends to become clairgustus.

Each of the intuitive levels of our five senses has its own psychic and spiritual phenomena. Clairvoyance includes spiritual vision, dreams, imagination, auric sight and such. It is a term often used to generically classify all psychic phenomena.

Clairaudience includes such phenomena as hearing spirit voices, music, telepathy, and comprehension of spiritual laws.

Clairsentience includes such phenomena as psychometry and healing.

---

1 Clairgustus is the term used by traditional spiritualism to describe the phenomena of psychic or spirit messages that come through fragrances and smells. The *gustus* comes from the Latin, meaning taste, so for our purposes, I will use the term clairaroma for psychic faculties associated with smell and clairgustus for psychic faculties associated with taste.

Clairgustus and clairaroma include the phenomena of idealism, discrimination, spiritual discernment, and higher imagination.

There is, of course, overlap, because our senses rarely operate under isolated conditions. As traditional spiritualists still do, it is feasible to use the term clairgustus for both smell and taste, since they are highly dependent upon each other. We often cannot taste food unless we smell it. For example, hold your nose and close your eyes while sampling a piece of onion and a piece of potato. You will not notice any difference, except maybe in texture.

The phenomena associated with each of these is much more expansive than what is described above. For anyone wishing to develop psychic and intuitive faculties, begin with the physical sense that is strongest for you. Do you respond more strongly to fragrances, sounds, images, touches, or tastes? As you develop it and its higher faculty, the other spiritual senses will also unfold.

It is not unusual to find those who see things wishing they could hear. Those who hear often wish they could see. Those who feel wish they could see or hear. It doesn't really matter. As you develop one, they all begin to unfold for you. Although you may initially only feel things or get vague impressions, as you hone that sensitivity, you will find that you also start to see, hear, smell, and taste as well.

We have probably all heard stories about individuals who lost one of their senses, and as a result one or more of the remaining senses became more attuned, as if to compensate for the loss. I graduated from high school with an individual who was blind. It was amazing what he could do through touch. He could almost literally see through his hands. If you went up to him and said nothing to him, he could usually tell who you were just by touching and feeling your arm.

Several years ago, I attended my class reunion. I had not seen my friend in at least 15 years. I didn't say a word to him, but placed my hand on his shoulder in greeting. He took my forearm in his hand and felt along it. It took him several moments, but then he spoke my name. His sense of touch accessed his old memory bank and brought the information forward.

Situations like this should remind us that everything we have experienced is in memory somewhere. It should also teach us that the subtlety of our senses and their abilities are much more far reaching than we give them credit for. Everything that we experience on any level— physical, emotional, mental, and spiritual—is mediated by the subconscious mind. If we learn to access it, we soon discover that there is much more going on around us on all levels than we may be conscious of.

One of the intuitive faculties easiest to develop is clairsentience. When we look at the human body from a sensory perspective, it is not difficult to understand this. The skin is our largest sensory organ. It is the outer covering to the body. It protects while also serving as a sensory system. It also is a symbol of our continuing ability to develop our higher faculties throughout our life, as the cells of the skin are continually regenerating.

Our body is continually giving off and absorbing energy fields with which it interacts. In metaphysics, this is called the human aura. The human body is a wondrous mechanism. It gives off sound, light, electricity, magnetics, electromagnetics, and other energies as well. It also has the ability to respond to all of these energies.

The subconscious mind monitors and mediates all of this interaction. If you have ever had unexplained feelings of uneasiness in places you have walked into, or have had individuals with whom you instantly click, you have experienced how these energy exchanges occur. How this applies specifically to psychometry will be elaborated upon in more detail in the next chapter.

One of the specific expressions of clairsentience is psychometry. Psychometry translates as soul measuring. It is the ability to sense impressions from objects, persons, and places, about events previous to the encounter.

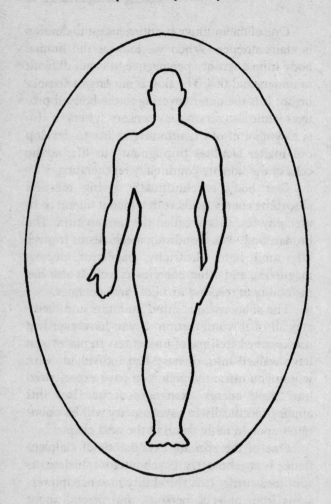

The Human Aura

By touching the object, the person, or by being in a place, you receive messages or information, but it is not attained simply through the sense of touch. This sense, however, becomes a bridge between ordinary sensory perception to the more intuitive.

There are basically two kinds of imprints left on objects and places. The first is a personal imprint. In this type, an individual's experiences are imprinted on an object. It may be a single experience or a series of experiences.

The second type is a gathered or group imprint. In this type, you receive impressions of everyone who has touched or handled the object, or who may have passed through or lived in a particular place. This type of imprint is what often makes reading an antique difficult. The images can be so plentiful and varied that they come out jumbled.

There is often an emotional coloring to what is felt or experienced. Most psychic and/or intuitive impressions are strongest when there is an emotional impulse associated with it. The personal object or place has been charged with the emotions of the individual or the events of the place. Emotions magnetize, or imprint, the object or place with events surrounding them. How this occurs specifically will be explored in the next chapter.

The intensity of the emotion surrounding the object or place determines, to a great degree, how strongly information can be attuned to and perceived. Places of traditional hauntings are usually locations in which intensely emotional (often negative) events occurred. The uneasiness people feel in this situation is the negative emotions imprinted by events in the lives of the people who lived there.

Periodically, I am asked to confer in criminal investigations, such as in the case of missing children. In such cases, I prefer to know as little about the situation as possible so as not to color my own impressions. I also require a photo of the individual, an article of clothing, or favorite toy that has not been washed or cleaned since the incident occurred. These will still carry the energy imprint of the individual. This facilitates linking with any emotions, positive or negative, in regards to events in the individual's life at the time. By touching the object, I can be in the vicinity of the person without having actually touched him or her.

The greatest difficulty for me in situations such as this is disconnecting from what I have perceived because the emotions and circumstances are so intense. Part of what this book will teach you is how to control your psychic sense of touch. You will learn to turn it on and off at will. More of these processes and other uses will be examined later in the text.

Attuning to the object or place and the energy associated with it is a lot like rewinding and

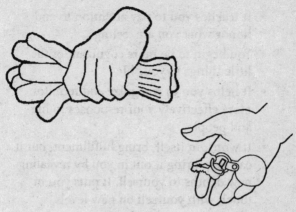

Psychometry

Psychometry is an aspect of clairsentience. It is the ability to detect something about a person or event through the sense of touch. If you have ever held an item of a person's clothing or jewelry and felt you knew something about the person's character, surroundings or influence, you've experienced psychometry.

replaying a tape. Often, the reproduction can be quite accurate and faithful to the events imprinted upon the object. Information may come through that provides great assistance. The messages, though, may also be colored by the personality of the individual receiver and may only contain partial information. With psychometry, the subconscious translates the imprint of the object and recreates a copy of it for the conscious mind.

Developing clairsentience, and specifically psychometry, has many benefits:

- It teaches you to pay attention to and honor what you are feeling.
- You begin to be more cognizant of the little things in your life.
- It helps you to recognize and monitor more effectively your responses to life and people.
- It won't, in itself, bring fulfillment, but it can help bring it out in you by revealing new depths to yourself. It puts you in touch with yourself on new levels.
- It helps you to develop the art of concentration.
- It helps you to focus and recall details otherwise missed. Most miss a great deal of life because they don't observe what they see and experience. Look how often observers of an accident will have differing versions of what occurred.
- It helps us to close down or shift away from the conscious mind to open ourselves to more creative possibilities.

EXERCISES

I: Questionnaire: Are you clairsentient?

Clairsentience is the ability to get impressions from people, objects, places. If you can answer "yes" to any of the questions that follow, you are clairsentient. The more yes answers there are, the stronger the faculty within you. Regardless of how strong or weak, even the least ability can be developed and honed for psychometry.

1. Have you ever felt someone's eyes on you without actually seeing them, or when, in fact, you are alone?

2. Have you ever felt someone's presence before actually seeing them?

3. Have you ever had a deja vu or "I've been here before" experience? (Also refer to Exercise III in this chapter.)

4. Do certain rooms or people make you feel more comfortable or uncomfortable?

5. Have you ever sensed correctly the mood of a spouse, friend, or lover without any verbal communication?

6. Do you find yourself easily caught up in the moods of others?

7. Are you able to know whether you like or dislike someone when you meet them for the first time?

8. Have you ever walked into a room and felt that something (such as an argument or a fight) had gone on before you arrived without being told?

9. Do you have what is called "a way with animals"?

10. Upon meeting someone for the first time, can you sense what kind of childhood he or she had?

11. Are you a touchy-feely kind of person?

12. Do you dislike other people touching you or coming too much into your space?

13. Do you find that your truest first impressions about people come not from their appearance, but from their handshake?

14. Is the soundness of your sleep disturbed by the position of your bed? Does your head have to be toward magnetic north for you to sleep well?

15. Can you tell if something of yours is "out of place" before actually seeing or discovering it?

II: Having fun with outside communications

One of the easiest ways of testing and developing your clairsentient ability is through communications that come to you. It is also enjoyable and causes no harm. It can be a non-threatening way to test yourself.

The next time a letter comes from a friend, before opening it, take a few deep breaths and allow yourself to relax. Rub your hands briskly together to heighten their sensitivity. (You may even choose to perform one or more of the exercises described in Chapter Four.) Close your eyes and hold the letter between your hands or against your forehead. Then ask yourself some basic questions:

What is the general tone or mood of the letter writer? Is it good news or bad? What emotions do you personally experience as you hold it? Does anything else come to mind?

Eventually you will find yourself becoming more and more accurate at picking up and perceiving the tone and contents of such communications. You will begin to surprise yourself.

Try the same thing the next time the phone rings. Take a deep breath and relax. Then place your hand on top of the phone and let it ring once or twice while your hand is on it. Mentally ask yourself some questions about the caller as you do:

Is it male or female? Is it someone I know or a stranger? What is the call about?

Keep it simple. You will find that if you trust your first impressions, you will begin to develop a fairly high degree of accuracy. If you become confident with it, you can even answer the phone using the caller's name— "Hi, Donna."

The worst that can happen is that you're wrong. And if that makes you uncomfortable or embarrasses you, you can always make up some excuse for doing it, such as, "I'm sorry, I thought you were Donna. She was supposed to call me right back."

III: *I've been here before*

Deja Vu, or "I've been here before" feelings, are not uncommon. Many people experience them with varying intensity. Sometimes, the feelings and impressions are so strong that it is comparable to being transferred back to another place and time, complete with all the decor. At other times, it may simply be a vague, undefined feeling of familiarity.

Feelings of the "I've been here before" variety are often produced by accidentally tuning into a new place and then finding they coincide with feelings within our memory. We relate what we are experiencing from the surroundings to something more familiar with us in our present life. That memory may be a picture of something we saw in school, or from a dream, or from a variety of sources. Discerning whether it is a true deja vu experience or something you are relating to from your present life can be difficult.

Even if we cannot discern, the most important part is realizing that your own, natural clairsentience is operating. What you are picking up from the environment is the trigger for the "I've been here before" feelings. Whether it relates to a past life, or to something you have experienced more recently, isn't what you should focus on initially. Focus on the fact that your body and your senses have picked up impressions from the environment.

Seeing Through Touch ❦ 21

Recognizing this alone can be a wonderful tool for us. As we begin to recognize that this is occurring, we can use it to learn about many places we visit. As you focus your attention on what you are feeling, rather than trying to understand and discern it all, you will become even more sensitive to those feelings that are impinging upon you from the environment.

Don't try to focus on details. Initially, you may only get general impressions. You may simply have an idea of a particular emotion, or issue, or event with no definable facts. Through practicing many of the exercises in this book, this will become stronger.

Relax and experience what you are feeling. Do not force it.

Do not worry if images of the present arrive. They may simply be, and often are, images that the subconscious is using to help you understand what you are experiencing. It can be a way of helping you establish some parameters for relating.

Ask yourself some simple questions, and trust your first impression. Pay attention to which way you feel as you ask them: Have those who lived here been happy or sad? Do you feel comfortable or uncomfortable? Warm or cold?

Run through the senses, and assess your emotional response to the place. Breathe, deeply through the nose. How do you feel when you smell the place? Does the sound of your voice or the voices of others stimulate a response? Stand in different places and look the place over with your eyes. Do some views seem more comfortable or pleasant to you? Do your emotions change? Also, as you stand in different places, close your eyes, and ask yourself how you feel: happy? sad? warm? cold?

Record anything that you feel or experience—even if it doesn't make sense. Recording it often triggers greater clarification. It helps pull the information out of that vague ethereal realm and crystallize it in your own mind. Occasionally, you may even wish to record why you think you felt the way you did. Let the imagination run, even if it seems an outrageous possibility and that you are "making it up." You may discover there is more to your imaginings than you thought possible. If it does nothing else, it develops more flexibility in the mind, and it sends a message to the subconscious that you are ready for even greater perceptions.

At some point you may even wish to study the location or building to discover the veracity of your impressions. Asking residents in the area is helpful. Going to the library or city records may also provide input. Don't be discouraged if nothing turns up. It doesn't mean that you were wrong. There just may be no record of it.

❦

❦ 2 ❦

How Psychometry Works

Psychometry literally means "soul measuring." It is the ability to read part or all of an object's history or the history of those people who may have handled it. While it deals most often with the past, it may often reflect present states as well.

There is, occasionally, disagreement among individuals who practice psychometry as to whether it can be used to read or reflect the future. This depends entirely on one's perspective. The object will not hold impressions of the future, as they will not have occurred yet. On the other hand, someone who is capable of seeing the pattern of the past in the life of the individual through the object can usually make very viable predictions based on that data. This is because most people never change their patterns.

There are three kinds of psychometry, all of which will be explored to some extent in this book. They overlap often, as there are not always clearly defined borders. They are:

- Object Psychometry
- Location Psychometry

- Person Psychometry

Object Psychometry is probably the most common, and the form most people are familiar with. Every object has its own energy and is often imprinted by the owner of that object in a unique manner. How this occurs is part of what we will explore in this chapter.

In this form of psychometry, you learn to establish a rapport with the object and the energies imprinted upon it. Most often, the touching of objects to read their imprints occurs in one of three ways:

- Held in the hands.
- Placed against the forehead and/or face.
- Placed against the solar plexus.

These are points on the body where our chakra centers are most active for sensory impression through psychometry. Chakras are points in the body where there is a higher degree of energy activity. They control all energy going into and emanating from the body. The seven major chakras are points of greater electromagnetic activity in and around the body. Two of these are the points of the brow and the solar plexus. The hands are also points of great energy activity.

By holding the object in the hands or placing the object against the forehead or face, impres-

Examples of psychic touching

sions are received about the owner of the object or events surrounding the object's history. "This is based on the theory that emotional events create a thin film that coats all objects, including people, in the immediate vicinity of the occurrence. This coating of objects or people is permanent. A psychometrist coming in contact with such objects or individuals will be able to read the coating substance and thus will be able to reconstruct the emotional event."[2]

There is a growing interest in the metaphysical field in using psychometry in detective work. Objects are connecting links to the owner, or owners, and the important events associated with them. They are also links to events and situations

2 Holzer, Hans. *The Truth About ESP.* Manor Books, Inc.; New York, 1975, pg. 46.

associated with places important and significant to the owner(s).

This has application in many areas. Two of the most common are archaeology and criminal investigations. In archaeological psychometry, the individual reads, or attunes to, a historical object or site and is impressed with the history of events and people surrounding it. This can provide further information and insight into historical periods.

In criminal investigations, it has application in a variety of ways. Location of lost or stolen items, murder, and missing people are just a few areas. My personal experience has centered mostly around missing and abused children. A connecting link to the individual is required. Clothing, picture, jewelry, hair sample, etc. is used to establish rapport or alignment with the individual or events critical in the life of the individual. Methods for doing this will be elaborated upon in Chapter Five.

The difficulty in this application of psychometry lies in proper discrimination. Psychic information is just that—psychic. It is not always verifiable. Accusations and proclamations must be couched with great care, as it is easy to destroy the lives of innocent individuals with inappropriate or unfounded accusations.

Location psychometry relates strongly to deja vu, or "I've been here before," kinds of feelings.

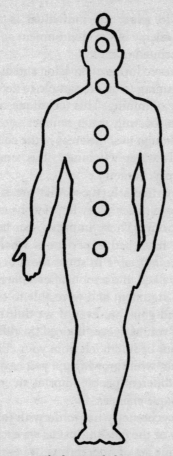

The human chakra system

The seven chakras are points of greater electromagnetic emana-
tions from and around the body. The palms of the hands are also
points of greater energy activity. The hands, the brow and the
solar plexus are places of greater "touch sensitivity."

By learning to relax, the individual is able to attune to the energy of the environment and what has been imprinted upon it.

This relates to forms of dowsing and divining, such as in attuning to an ore sample to determine the feasibility of mining. This technique can also be helpful in locating water sources, ores, and minerals. Although in some areas of the country it is still called "water witching," it is simply an extension of psychometry.

Events, particularly those that are strongly emotional, leave traces. They imprint the location where they occur. These imprints can be read. Most people have had experiences where they have felt uncomfortable in some room or home. We have all walked into a room after someone has had a heated argument and were able to tell that something had gone on, even if we didn't know the details. If you have ever noticed the difference in the way your bedroom felt from your children's or your parents' while growing up, you have experienced how different people imprint an environment with unique energies.

Person psychometry has to do with the individual energy of the person. Just as we each have our own unique set of fingerprints, we each have our unique energy field. Person psychometry is used by everyone. How often are we able to assess the mood of someone without speaking to them?

When we meet someone for the first time, are we instantly attracted or repelled? We may not know why these impressions occur, but they often register quite strongly.

The ability to attune to and assess where an individual is at is part of what can be developed with this form. This can be used in healing work from a variety of perspectives. It can be developed into a form of X-ray clairvoyance. It can be used to develop empathic healing techniques, some of which will be discussed in Chapter Six. It can be used to locate weaknesses and strengths in the body and the energy field surrounding it. (Keep in mind, though, that only a trained physician has the legal right to diagnose illness and disease.)

The imprint of objects and locations can be purposeful or accidental. An example of purposeful imprint with objects and places can be seen in the creation of talismans and charms charged with a particular energy to affect a particular result. Churches, temples, and meditation rooms are places where efforts are made to create an atmosphere of reverence and peace. Simply by entering the space, you feel more relaxed. They facilitate the achievement of altered states and such.

Accidental imprints are much more common. An object held in your possession for long periods of time becomes magnetized or imprinted with your energy. It happens automatically. Many church holy relics were simply imprinted by the various saints and holy ones accidentally, not through any purposeful design. They became charged with the energy of the individual by simply having been a part of the individual's life. In the same way our favorite pieces of jewelry become more strongly imprinted.

The rooms we spend the most time in carry the strongest imprints. Someone walking through your house for the first time should have little trouble in determining which room or rooms you spend little time in.

Places and objects where intensely emotional events occur are more strongly imprinted. Many haunted homes are not truly haunted by ghosts, but by the imprints of events of the previous residents. The "spirit," the imprints, of the previous residents haunt the home. This is why some homes have a wonderful warm feeling about them, and others may not.

It is also why it takes a while for you to feel comfortable when you first move into a new home. Your furnishings and your presence must override the previous imprints. When your spirit begins to fill the place, it begins to truly feel like home. You imprint the space and the objects within it with your own emotional energies.

Two Theories on Psychometry

Although there are a variety of theories as to how psychometry works, two seem the more probable, particularly to our more modern scientific minds:

- The Aura Theory of Psychometry
- The Hologram Theory

The Aura Theory of Psychometry is based upon the concept that all matter has an energy field surrounding it. Anything that has an atomic structure will have an aura. Every atom of every substance is comprised of electrons and protons that are in constant motion. These electrons and protons are electrical and magnetic energy vibrations. The atoms that comprise animate matter are more active and vibrant than those of inanimate matter.

The human body is a wondrous mechanism. It gives off and responds to a wide variety of energies—including light, sound, electricity, magnetism, electro-magnetics, and thermal. The aura surrounding it is vibrant and strong, and in the average individual, it usually extends eight to ten feet out around the body in all directions.

There are two characteristics of the aura that relate directly to psychometry. (For information on all the qualities and characteristics of the aura, you may wish to consult my earlier work, *How to See and Read the Aura*.) The first is that our individual aura will interact with the auras of other people and the energy fields of the plant, animal, and mineral kingdoms.

Because of the strong electromagnetic make-up of our aura, we are constantly giving off (electrical) and absorbing (magnetic) energy. Anything with an atomic structure can be imprinted upon. Our own aura can leave an imprint on everything with which it interacts. This can be another person, a part of the environment, or even an object.

It is this electromagnetic aspect which magnetizes objects and places. We leave energy traces of a frequency unique to us wherever we go. If you are used to sitting in a particular chair, you magnetize it with your energy. Think about the first time you took a seat in a new class. On subsequent sessions, you usually return to that same spot. It becomes increasingly more comfortable. You build your energy around that spot.

If for some reason, you return and find someone else in that seat, you find yourself uncomfortable in any new spot you must take. It is because you left an imprint on that seat—in that area. It is why your room at home feels different from the rooms of others' in the house. We imprint the space with our own energy.

Your aura charges the environment with an energy pattern in resonance with your own frequency. The breaking-in period of beds, clothes, new homes is nothing more than the time it takes for

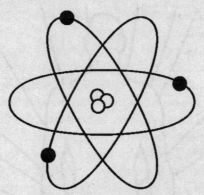

The energy vibrations of atoms.

your aura to magnetize and harmonize the environment or object with your own energy frequencies.

A child's blanket or favorite stuffed toy becomes imprinted or magnetized with the energy unique to the child. The toy or blanket, because of its atomic structure, has the capability of absorbing the energy given off by the child. Holding the blanket or toy is a way for the child to recharge and balance. The blanket or toy serves as an energy reservoir that the child can draw upon.

Some objects absorb energies more easily than others. They also can be attuned to more easily, and may also dissipate their imprints more quickly. Cotton and natural fabrics are more easily imprinted than synthetics. Prayer shawls and meditation blankets are examples of this. In detective work, articles of clothing are powerful

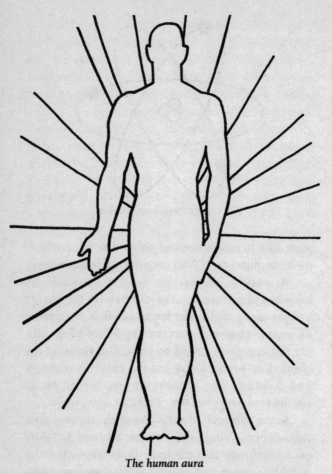

The human aura

There are a variety of energy fields and emanations surrounding and emanating from the human body. These comprise a major part of the auric field. One of the strongest aspects of the human aura is its electro-magnetic quality.

tools to align with the owner, as long as the articles have not been washed. Water is an excellent conductor of electricity, and it can cleanse the article of the energy charge that has accumulated within it. This is why children hate having their favorite blanket or stuffed toy washed.

Metals are also excellent conductors of electricity. Objects that are metal are more easily imprinted, which is why they are often used in the construction of talismans and charms. Because of their conducting ability, the energies imprinted upon them are also more easily detected by the psychometrist. Metal objects, though, can also dissipate their charge more quickly.

Wood objects are more difficult to magnetize, but they will also retain that imprint much longer. It may require more sensitivity by the psychometrist to attune to the energies imprinted on wooden objects.

The basis of psychometry is the direct result of the interaction of the individual's aura upon objects, places, and people. The longer the person has had contact with an object or place, the stronger it becomes charged with an energy pattern similar to that of the person. A sensitive person can then hold the object or enter an environment and become impressed with insights into the individual to whom it belongs or to important events surrounding it.

The Hologram Theory of Psychometry has to do with new paradigms and studies in brain functions and how they relate to transcendent experiences. It also has ties to quantum physics.

Neurosurgeon Karl Pribram did pioneering research at Stanford University in regards to brain function paradigms. His research led him to conclude that the brain operates in many ways like a hologram. "A hologram is a special type of optical storage system that can best be explained by an example: if you take a holographic photo of, say, a horse, and cut out one section of it, e.g. the horse's head, and then enlarge that section to the original size, you will get, not a big head, but a picture of the whole horse. In other words, each individual part of the picture contains the whole picture in condensed form. The part is in the whole and the whole is in each part — a type of unity-in-diversity and diversity-in-unity."[3] The key point is simply that the part has access to the whole.

Thus, any piece of the hologram will reconstruct the whole. What this means can be extended to the study of psychometry. Theoretically, any piece of our life, or anything touched by us, would carry an imprint that can be used to connect directly with us on some level. These connections are called in radionics and psionics "witnesses."

3 Wilber, Ken, Ed. *The Holographic Paradigm*. New Science Library; Boulder, Co. 1982, p. 2.

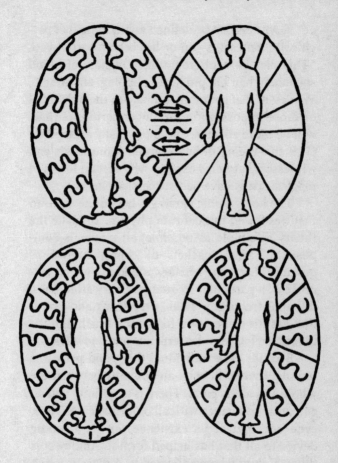

Energy exchange through the aura

Because of its electromagnetic aspects, the human aura can imprint itself, magnetize, or leave traces of itself on objects, places, and people.

A witness can be defined as anything that psychically represents you or has been a part of you. "This can be a photograph, a signature, blood specimen, hair clipping, nail clipping, anything."[4] Witnesses that are more intimate to the individual or those in possession for longer periods of time, will be more effective and more easily attuned to. (It is this theory of holographic connections and witnesses that helps explain why certain forms of magical spells have had successful effects.)

The holographic paradigm has connections to theories found in quantum physics. To make the theory as simple as possible, all matter is composed of small packets of energy known as quanta. This energy makes up atoms which resonate at a particular frequency. Every atom has a different frequency. Thus, everything and everyone has his or her own frequency, much like the difference found in fingerprints and snowflakes.

Because each individual thing and person is unique, there will exist an empathy between the whole and all its parts. There is an affinity and an empathic resonance with all of its make up. Thus, even one part of its existence can be a tuning device to all that has helped form it. An object is thus a link to whoever owned it. A place is a link to whoever and whatever occurred within it.

---

4 Cosimano, Charles. *Psionics 101*. Llewellyn Publications, St. Paul, 1987, p.82.

Physicist David Bohm's work with subatomic physics and quantum potential led him to conclude that physical entities which seemed to be separate were actually linked in this unique, underlying fashion.[5]

These theories of holograms and quantum physics help account for transcendent experiences such as anything within the psychic realm, including psychometry and even past lives. To truly understand this more effectively, we have to examine how the brain functions.

Traditionally, we have explored the idea that the brain has two ways of seeing, each based on the different characteristics of the individual hemispheres. Each hemisphere gathers information, but handles it differently.

One, often the dominant left, has a tendency to take over and inhibit the other half. The left hemisphere analyzes, counts time, verbalizes, and is logical and linear in its approach to life. On the other hand, a second way of knowing and learning is capable through the right hemisphere. Through it we intuit, imagine, see relationships, and have leaps of insight.

The holographic super-theory of brain functioning says "that our brains mathematically construct 'hard' reality by interpreting frequencies from a dimension transcending time and

_____
5 Wilber, Ibid. p. 2

space. The brain is a hologram, interpreting a holographic universe....Psychic phenomena are only by-products of this simultaneous-every-where matrix...."[6] Implied within this is the concept of hemispheric synchronization. While the left brain is constructing and analyzing the hard reality, the right brain should be functioning to interpret it.

A third way of knowing comes through this balanced operation of left and right brain hemispheres. It is called hemispheric synchronization. When the hemispheres of the brain are balanced and operating together, we assimilate information more easily. We also learn more quickly, and we retain conscious control of higher perceptions, including those of the psychic nature. It is very probable that through balancing the hemispheres of the brain, the holographic operation is facilitated.

The hologram theory enriches and enlarges traditional concepts of brain functioning. It makes sense of phenomena that had once been scoffed at. It does not negate what we know about the brain, but it elaborates how we know, and more importantly, how we can perceive and know even more. It is this hologram functioning which explains the human ability to have mystical experiences and experience psychic phenomena.

---

6 Ferguson, Marilyn, "Karl Pribram's Changing Reality." in Ken Wilber, Ed. *The Holographic Paradigm*, pp. 22-23.

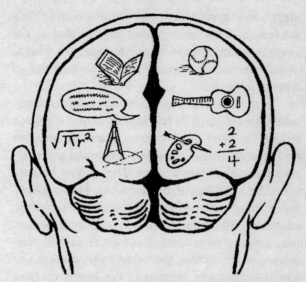

The two hemispheres of the brain

Traditionally, the brain was looked at as having two ways of knowing, based upon functions of the two hemispheres. Recently, a third way of knowing, probably based on a unified functioning of the hemispheres, has arisen. This is the hologram brain-functioning. It transcends the traditional ways of "knowing."

Everything is connected and a part of us knows this—at least on some occasions.

When we develop our awareness and learn to shift from our normal ways of thinking—when we utilize both hemispheres of the brain—we have greater ability to shift into holographic perceptions. We can attune to things distant from us, but related to us. We can hold an object and shift our consciousness to what it was once connected to. This holographic functioning of the brain is more perceptive and operates on dimensions beyond our conventional perspectives of time and space.

In the Western world, the left brain is dominant. We are often overly logical in our approach to life. We deny, or play down, the more intuitive and creative side of ourselves controlled primarily through right brain activity. This is why balance must be established between the hemispheres. Involvement in meditation or creative activities, stimulates the right brain into greater functioning, helping to balance the logical side of ourselves. As we do this, the holographic perceptions are automatically triggered. We begin to have transcendent experiences beyond those of our physical five senses. Our natural psychic perceptions awaken.

This is also why it is important to acknowledge any mystical or psychic experience. It affirms the reality of this third manner of functioning of the brain. It reinforces it. It then is able to become stronger. The more we recognize, acknowledge and use it, the more powerful it becomes for us.

EXERCISES

IV: *Shifting consciousness*

A creative person is one who can process information and perceptions in new ways. In order to do this, we have to learn to shift out of our usual way of thinking and perceiving. We have to establish a more direct link with the subconscious mind, because it is the source of all of our subtle perceptions.

For most people in the Western world, there is difficulty shifting from the normal left brain activity to our more creative and intuitive perceptions. In fact, for most people, the left brain is frequently over-stimulated. If you don't believe this, some simple observations of your own thought processes will prove it.

Pay attention to your thought processes the next time you leave your work environment. After a hectic day at work, most people's minds are running rampant. You are looking at things from this angle, that angle, putting it down, picking it up, going over it again and again. Whenever this occurs, it reflects excessive left brain activity. The left hemisphere is over-stimulated.

The guidelines in this section, and the other exercises which follow in this chapter, are designed to help stimulate right brain activity and balance it with the left.

Develop your ability to relax: Relaxation is the key to shifting consciousness. This includes physical and mental relaxation. For most people, the physical relaxation is usually easier to accomplish than the mental and emotional, so begin with it. Most people hold emotional and mental tension somewhere in the body. As you learn to relax the physical body, emotional and mental tension is also alleviated.

Assume a seated or prone position, one in which you are comfortable. Practice sending warm soothing sensations to each and every part of the body. Start with the feet and move up to the head. Take your time with this.

To assist the process, alternately tense and relax each part before focusing and sending the warm, soothing sensations. This helps to loosen and alleviate stress and tension being held specifically in each part of the body.

Do not be discouraged if it takes a while initially. If you are not used to relaxing, it must be learned just like anything else. With persistence and practice, you will find areas of your body in which you hold tension more strongly, and so you will know where to focus your efforts. You will eventually find that it will become easier and faster to relax.

For psychometry, or the expression of any psychic ability, great depths of relaxation are not necessary. Effective altered states of consciousness only require light states of relaxation and ease.

Practice and use rhythmic breathing: Breathing is essential to life. Fresh air and proper breathing are necessary for a relaxed and balanced mind and body. This is even more effective when combined with the progressive relaxation. When we are tense, our breathing pattern is very different from when we are relaxed.

Breathing should always be done from the diaphragm. Many people also have a bad habit of only mouth breathing, not realizing that nostril breathing is more natural, balanced and healthy. The nostril and nasal passages contain hair which filter the air. The mucous membranes also serve to warm the air. This makes the air fit for the delicate organs of the lungs and more relaxing to the body.

Alternate nostril breathing is a yoga method for vitalizing and relaxing. It balances the hemi-spheres of the brain, and energizes and balances the polarities of the body. It enhances our ability to learn and assimilate information. Performing it prior to meditation, psychic practices or simply studying, makes the time spent in such activities more effective.

Alternate nostril breathing developed out of yoga based on the concept of polarities in the body. The energy of the body, mind and spirit has polarity within it. This is expressed predomi-nantly through two ancient Hermetic principles:

- Principle of Polarity: "Everything is Dual; everything has poles; everything has its pair of opposites; like and unlike are the same; opposites are identical in nature, but different in degree; extremes meet; all truths are but half truths; all paradoxes may be reconciled."[7]

- Principle of Gender: "Gender is in everything; everything has its Masculine and Feminine principles; gender manifests on all planes."[8]

In yoga, the moon, or feminine breath, is called Ida, and the sun, or masculine breath, is called Pingala. The balance of the two is Susumna. Our energy has polarity—positive and negative, electrical and magnetic, masculine and feminine, sun and moon. Even the hemispheres of the brain can be categorized in this manner. The left hemisphere is masculine and the right is feminine. The balance of the two breaths creates a balance of the two hemispheres. This increases practical intuition and shifts us to the holographic perception that facilitates transcendent experiences of all kinds.

The basic technique is comprised of alternate breaths, breathing in one nostril and then out the

---

7 Three Initiates, *The Kybalion*. Yogi Publication Society; Chicago, 1940, p. 32.

8 Ibid.

other. Conscious attention to the tip of your nose, particularly during the in-breath, will greatly enhance the effects of this exercise.

Assume a seated position, and place your thumb and fingers of your right hand over your nose and exhale. Also place your tongue against the roof of your mouth, just behind your front teeth. This serves to connect two primary channels or meridians of energy in the body. (Meridians in Eastern philosophy can be likened to nerve pathways within the body. Two of these are most important. They are called the governing meridian and the conception meridian. They run up the spine and central median of the body. These two energy pathways are critical to the balance of polarities and hemispheric activity of the brain.)

Using your thumb, close your right nostril and inhale for a slow count of four through the left nostril. Keeping the right nostril closed, clamp your fingers over the left, pinching the entire nose closed. Hold your breath for a count of 10.

Now release your thumb, opening your right nostril, but keeping the left closed with your fingers. Exhale slowly for a count of six to eight out through the right nostril.

Now release your nose entirely, and with the thumb of your left hand, close off the left nostril. Inhale through the right for a slow count of four. Then clamp your fingers over the right nostril, so that the thumb and fingers have pinched the nose closed entirely. Hold your breath for a count of 10-16, as before. Then release your thumb, and exhale out the left nostril for a count of six to eight, while keeping the right nostril closed with your fingers.

Repeat this with four to five breaths, alternating each side. Breathe in one nostril, hold and exhale out the other. Reverse it and repeat the procedure.

Develop your ability to meditate: Meditation is a powerful, wonderful tool to assist shifting consciousness. Meditation doesn't mean that you have to sit with your back straight and your legs twisted into a lotus posture. It does mean that you have to calm the body and the mind so that you can perceive on deeper, more subtle levels.

The key to shifting your awareness, the manner in which you perceive the world, is using an altered state of consciousness. We have all experienced altered states. Dreaming is an altered state. So is daydreaming. Reading often takes you out of yourself. Even jogging, long drives, and listening to music will produce shifts in consciousness. Through meditation, you learn to shift in a controlled manner, you learn to consciously access the subconscious mind and direct its perceptive abilities along the lines we choose.

Most meditative techniques, regardless of their purpose, are simple. Anyone with practice

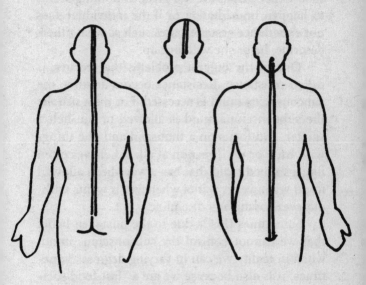

Governing and conception meridians

These two meridians are critical to the balance of polarity in the body. The governing is masculine, and the conception is the feminine. When balanced through techniques such as alternate nostril breathing, the hemispheres of the brain synchronize and altered states of perception are enhanced and more easily controlled.

and a little time can develop the ability. Unfortunately, most people are easily discouraged, or their expectations are too great. If nothing seems to happen immediately, or if the individual does not experience ecstatic states such as what others describe, he or she will give up.

One of the biggest problems that occurs, is called resistance. Resistance occurs anytime the subconscious mind is accessed. For most people, the subconscious mind is allowed to run helter skelter, and focus on a thousand and one things with little or no direction at all. It behaves often like a spoiled child that has always been allowed to do whatever it wants whenever it wants without ever having any discipline.

Sometimes this is due to the mistaken belief that we cannot control the subconscious mind, when in reality we can in varying degrees. Sometimes, it is also because we are a "fast-food society." We like everything instantly and quickly. We want to pull up to the drive-through window, pick up our stuff, and drive on. This includes our psychic development. When it doesn't work that way, individuals get discouraged.

Usually what happens, though, is the individual has difficulty focusing and concentrating. The person relaxes and begins to focus on a single idea or image, and the mind begins to wander. You start thinking about what you did at work, what someone said to you, how your friends are behaving, a thousand and one things.

This is actually a positive sign. Resistance only occurs when you have accessed the subconscious mind. It is important to recognize this and not be upset by it. It is also why learning to focus on a seed image or idea is beneficial to developing the ability to meditate. If your mind wanders, you simply bring it back to that seed point of focus.

Initially, you may find your mind wandering 80 to 90 times. Each time, though, that you recognize it and calmly return it back to your point of focus, you send a message to the subconscious. You are telling it that it is no longer all right to wander wherever it wishes. You are telling it to stay focused on what you decide. As you do this, eventually you will find it wandering less and less through your meditations. You are asserting discipline and control over the most powerful aspects of the mind. This process can take time and be difficult, but everyone can achieve some results almost immediately.

The key to its application in psychometry lies in developing two abilities: visualization and concentration. Visualization is the ability to create a mental picture and hold it steady within the mind. It can also have to do with holding a particular idea and all things associated with it in your mind, i.e., joy and all that joy would mean and add to your life. As you learn to visualize in your meditations, you will enhance your ability to perceive through focus in psychometry.

Concentration is the art of holding an image or idea strongly within your mind without wandering to other things. In psychometry, this is essential to being able to attune to and hold images and impressions central to the object, place, or person being psychometrized. With practice, we can all learn to hold a concentrated focus to the exclusion of others.

Try counting slowly to 10. Visualize each number in your mind, and hold that number to the exclusion of any other thought, until the next number is counted. I have often used this exercise in my development classes to teach visualization and concentration — and to demonstrate that it is not as easy as it seems. I rarely count at a regular speed. If other thoughts arise in the midst of the visualizing and concentration, even such thoughts as "Oh, this isn't so difficult," more practice is needed.

V: *Optical illusions*

Optical illusions often demonstrate that seeing is not always believing. Many people assume that only what they experience tangibly is all that is real. Optical illusions reflect the illusory phenomena of a fourth dimension of experiences.

With optical illusions, the eyes are able to see all of the inherent images. The eyes receive the information, which the optic nerve then codes and sends to the brain. As the information passes to the brain, the codes become more abstract and complex. The more complex the image, the more the brain has to work to understand what is being perceived. If it can't be understood through one part of the brain, another tries to translate and make sense of the images.

Playing with optical illusions helps us to shift consciousness. We trick the brain into new levels of perception. We begin to observe and contemplate what is not. It helps us to shift from our normal conscious mind perceptions to those that are more subtle and less tangible. They also help teach us that little is really known about how the brain processes information it receives through the eyes and the other senses.

Whatever meets the eyes, meets the brain. This holds for the other senses as well. We can use optical illusions to help us shift more quickly from left brain responses to right brain. Taking a few minutes to play with optical illusions will trigger right brain activity and even bring it into balance with the left brain. This facilitates the stimulation of the holographic level of perception through all of the senses, including touch.

This is especially true of irrational figures, dual images, or figure-ground illusions. Once the illusions are perceived, you will find the mind shifting from one image to the other. This shifting back and forth reflects both hemispheres operating to comprehend the total image, but each perceives and processes information differently. This shifting back and forth between images in the illusion creates hemispheric synchronization. The examples on the following pages reflects this shifting.

Take several minutes and study optical illusions. It helps you to shift from normal consciousness to that which is more transcendent. They make it easier to awaken your own psychic perceptions. It facilitates activating those parts of the brain and subconscious mind which has greater perception ability and which stimulate our own psychic ability. They awaken the realization of our ability to perceive on multiple levels. They develop unfocused observation which is a necessary tool for psychometry impressions.

Basic optical illusion
This optical illusion was drawn in the 1890s.
There are two different perceptions possible
within this illusion. Once they are both perceived,
the brain keeps shifting back and forth, from one
to another. This balances the hemispheres of the
brain. Your eyes and brain see it one way, then the
other. It is difficult to see the twins with the
puppy and the skull at the same time.

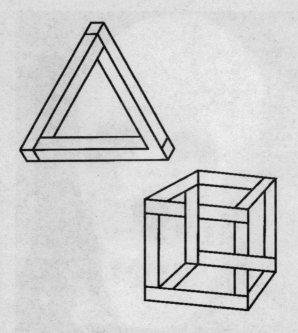

Irrational figures

Irrational figures only exist on paper and are not physically possible to construct. Because of their irrationality, they force the brain to shift from its normal, day-to-day processing (our rational approach to life) to try and perceive and understand on other levels, including a right brain approach to the information or even one that is more transcendent or psychic.

Figure-ground illusion

Do you see the letter "E"? This illusion occurs when your eyes can't choose between positive and negative shapes, since they are of equal intensity. Therefore, the eye repeatedly shifts from one area to another. This causes the processing of the information by the brain to repeatedly shift from the left hemisphere to the right.

Moiré pattern

When two or more geometric patterns of equally spaced repetitive elements are overlapped at certain angles, your brain and eyes fill in the intersections, producing a shimmer. This reflects a balanced working of right and left brain activity and can be used to shift the brain to levels of psychic perceptions simply by focusing on such patterns for several moments. This can be used as a preliminary warm-up for practicing psychometry.

❧ 3 ❧

The Basics
of Psychic Touch

For many people, psychometry is one of the easiest of the psychic abilities to develop. It is easily developed by everyone, and it can be used to hone and fine tune all of your psychic perceptions. Good psychometry requires specificity. Through the sense of touch, you can become consciously aware of circumstances relating to the object or about the people who have handled or possessed the objects.

The impressions may come in a variety of forms, but all occur through physical contact between the psychometrist and the object or person being attuned to. Often, the more recent impressions associated with the object, or those with the strongest emotional impact will be received first, although it doesn't always work that way. Do not be disheartened or discouraged if it doesn't do so for you. It simply means your energy and attunement may operate a little differently.

The four most common forms of impressions are:

- Physical
- Emotional
- Auditory
- Imagery

Physical impressions occur in a variety of ways. You may feel a tingling, an uneasiness, a change in temperature in yourself or in the object. Monitor your body. As you hold the object pay attention to whatever parts of your own body express themselves through sensation at that time. Do they itch, tingle? This often provides clues to physical aspects of the object's owner.

Many people initially will experience changes in temperature when they first hold the object. The object will become hot or cold, which gives the psychometrist a starting point. It is like shaking someone's hand for the first time. Whether it is limp or firm gives you a specific first impression of that person. Psychometry is similar. Pay attention to what you feel when you first touch the object or person.

Many of us psychometrize throughout the day without realizing it. Most of it occurs through accidental contact and touches. It also occurs so quickly that we don't always acknowledge it. Momentary handshakes often tell us "where an individual is at." Have you ever squirmed at someone's touch, not really knowing why it made you feel "icky?" Or, has someone touched you tenderly at times when you are stressed and it has been healing to you? Learning to pay more attention to these kinds of things is part of what this book will teach.

Emotional impressions are also easily received when holding or touching the object. Remember that emotional events and situations impress themselves strongly upon objects and places. Have you ever looked at someone or shaken their hand and known whether they were happy, sad, fun, depressed? Humans are very emotional beings, and we are more attuned to these than we often acknowledge.

When you hold an object, monitor your own emotional reactions. Do you start to feel tense, happy, silly, sad? Often, the emotions we experience are triggered by others around us. They are not our own. As you learn to monitor your own emotional responses, you also learn to control them more effectively. Part of this will be discussed later in Chapter Six.

This includes visions, symbols, scenarios, isolated pictures, and more. The pictures may be fragmented, scattered, or complete. It may simply come as a thought or idea about a certain scenario or event, or it may run like a movie through your mind.

Sometimes, the psychometrist may not actually see red, for example, but may simply think red is associated with what is being perceived. Honor and acknowledge it anyway. The subconscious mind may have attuned to the color red with this object, but sometimes people aren't visual. Then the images are brought forth to the conscious mind in the form of ideas or vague impressions of possible images without actually being seen.

The psychometrist may also experience a full blown *deja vu* experience. As the object is held, the entire area surrounding the psychometrist and the object seems to be transformed. The events are not being seen or experienced in the head, but in reality. It is as if the psychometrist is transported into the events themselves, perceiving them all first hand in their actual times and places. Although rare and more spontaneous, they do occur.

Sometimes you may have someone brush up against you accidentally and all kinds of strange thoughts and images will run through your head. Usually, we brush these aside, believing it's crazy to think or imagine such things. After all, there has never been any hint of this before. Those images may be actual or only symbolic, but in either case, they are very real and we need to honor them. We are sensing something, even if we don't understand it.

Oftentimes, images come in the form of symbols. Symbology is the only language of the subconscious mind. It is through images and symbols that it is able to communicate with the conscious mind. The images you sense or see while holding the object may be symbolic, rather than actual. Discerning the difference can be difficult, but with practice it becomes easier. Remember, the subconscious will send you images and symbols that it knows you have the ability to interpret. As the reader, it is your task to do so. Nothing is as aggravating and amateurish as having a reader give an image and symbol and ask, "Can you relate to this?" or "Do you understand this?" It usually reflects insecurity and lack of development and practice.

As the psychometrist, it is your task to interpret for the individual. Initially, in the development stages, this kind of questioning is necessary, but as you develop you will need to move past this. The end of the reading, as we will discuss, is the appropriate time to get feedback. Ways of presenting psychic information beneficially will come later.

Auditory impressions also come in a variety of ways. Although not as frequent, they do occur. It often depends on the level of psychic development in the individual, and his or her own natural propensity for auditory signals.

Auditory signals may come in the form of ringing, buzzing, words, phrases, and even entire messages. Some mediums use their spirit guides to gather information about the object and its owners. These spirit communications may come in the form of auditory perceptions.

Auditory perceptions may actually be heard in the mind alone, as if someone were speaking in your head. It may also come from outside of you, as someone would speak to you in real life. Sometimes the message is clear; other times it may be cryptic. It will be your responsibility to make sense of it for the person whose object is being read.

There are other ways messages from an object may come through. I often experience smells and fragrances with individuals. The smells and fragrances provide aromatic clues to the individual. For example, I may, while reading an object, start smelling eucalyptus. Since I know that eucalyptus is a fragrance that is calming to the emotions, it may very well indicate a lot of emotional stress and/or upheaval around the individual or even that it will be settling soon.

Occasionally, tastes may come through as well. For example, a heavy saccharin taste may signal diabetes.

As with all forms of psychism, practice and control are essential. The development of psychometry helps us in unfolding and controlling all of our psychic abilities. It helps us to overcome security in only the five senses. It teaches us to use altered states more effectively and practically. This helps us to assess people and situations in our life more effectively. Through developing psychometry, we are training ourselves to see larger patterns in life and the lives of those who touch us. We retrain ourselves to look at life and people from all levels of consciousness, not just what is visible to the naked eye.

Guidelines for Performing Psychometry

Relax and enjoy: Always approach the experience in a relaxed state. The development and use of psychometry is not a competition. You do not want to force or struggle with it. The experience is perfectly safe. See it as an adventure or an enjoyable game. If you cannot enjoy the unfolding, then do not do it.

Keep it simple: People often have misconceptions of anything dealing with the psychic. They see it as the "devil's work" or something shrouded in mystery. This perception is often promoted by individuals who perform their readings in poorly lit rooms with pungent incense. Psychometry can be developed very easily. You do not have to turn out the lights or use specific incenses, although they can be helpful to some people. You will need to remove distractions initially.

Keep an open mind: The greatest blocks to manifesting the innate psychic ability in all of us are fear and doubt. We often doubt the legitimacy of it, or we are afraid if we try we will be wrong. And if we are wrong, we may appear foolish. This is why working to develop it in a compatible group can be beneficial. Also, it is good to remember that a 20 percent accuracy rate is higher than the law of chance.

Work with a compatible group: In group situations, especially those working toward the same goal, there will be more positive reinforcement. You will be able to receive feedback, and you can help each other to hone and expand your abilities. The important thing to keep in mind with any group work is avoiding competition. Everyone's abilities are unique to him or her. Each must develop at his/her speed and in the manner best for him/her individually.

Keep a record: Write down dates and impressions you received, along with any other feedback or confirmations. You may even wish to keep track of personality influences, how you were feeling before and after. Your own record will prove to you that with practice your accuracy increases, as do the kinds of impressions.

Make preparations: Perform some kind of relaxation exercise. You may also choose to perform one or more of the touch enhancement exercises in the next chapter. Eliminate any distractions. Keep the phone off the hook. With time and practice your ability to focus and concentrate even amidst distractions will increase.

If you intend to do more than one psychometry reading, it is very beneficial to have a wet washcloth available. After completing each attunement, wipe your hands with the cloth. This washes off imprints left on the hands from the object. In this way, there will be no confusion when you move to the next object. If you touched an object to the face or forehead, you should wipe it also. You are literally and symbolically wiping the slate clean for truer and cleaner impressions from the new object.

Choose your object: This may already be done for you, or if you are in development, there may be a table in which objects to psychometrize are placed at each meeting by other members of the group.

It is nice to work on development in group situations, because then you have objects from people with whom you can check the accuracy of your impressions. Initially, use objects that have only been owned and used by one person. This helps eliminate confusion. Jewelry is good, and so are locks of hair. Photos are also good, particularly polaroid. Letters can also be psychometrized. Beginners should avoid antiques, as they will have been charged by many people. The impressions can be confusing.

Periodically, I do psychometry demonstrations for groups. At such times, I request that members of the audience place on a table at the front an object personal to them prior to my starting. Whenever possible, I try not to be in the room while this placement occurs. In this way, the reading is less likely to be prejudiced by my observation of the individual. I prefer knowing little or nothing about the individual whose object I am working with.

At the scheduled time, I enter. I have with me a wet washcloth to wipe my hands after each reading, so that the vibrations of the previous do not interfere with the present one.

I will choose an object from the table, look at it, touch it and hold it in my hands, and I may occasionally place it against my forehead. Sometimes my eyes are open; sometimes I keep them closed throughout the reading.

I am often asked how I know which object to start with. The answer is simple: It doesn't matter. Choose whichever one you are drawn to or which catches your eye.

Attune to the object: Begin by making a silent intention to gain impressions. It's a means of communicating to the subconscious mind exactly what you wish it to do for you.

Then, choosing your object, hold, touch, and examine it. Hold it between your hands. Place it against your cheek, forehead or solar plexus. Touch and handle it in the manner you feel comfortable with. Pay attention to how you choose to handle the object. If you usually handle objects with just your hands, and then find yourself wanting to place it against the solar plexus, this is a clue for you. It has significance.

Most good psychometrists begin by describing the object to the audience, if working in a group. If working one on one, he or she still will audibly describe and comment on the object itself. *This is essential.* Always start by describing the object itself.

This does several things for you. First, it helps create a mind-shift for you. It becomes an audible signal to the subconscious mind that you are ready to receive impressions. Second, it helps ease nervousness. Some people are good at receiving impressions, but they have difficulty in expressing them. Third, the mere act of describing it creates a triggering that helps release the flow of impressions from the subconscious that you have already received from handling the object.

The impressions usually flow for me immediately upon describing the object, and I begin to switch into what I am receiving. This is a common experience among psychometrists.

Observe first your body responses and initial emotions as you handle and describe the object. Do you feel good handling the object, or uncomfortable? Are there any tinglings anywhere? Pain?

Pleasure? Warmth? Cold? Also note the strongest emotions. Even if you cannot "feel" the emotion, ask yourself: "What is the strongest emotion associated with this object?" Then trust what comes to mind. Even though you may not be feeling it, that thought is very likely what your subconscious has picked up from you handling the object.

These first impressions often provide clues to the personality of the object's owner. Relate it to him/her. For example, "I am feeling weakness in the right knee and thus this person probably has a problem in this area. If it is not an actual physical problem, it is then symbolic of...." What you are feeling has some connection to the owner of the object—actual or symbolic. Either way, it is usually significant.

Give the impressions: Begin with the simple impressions, even if somewhat general. Describe what you are feeling, regardless of how obvious. What stands out most strongly for you? Be brief and balanced. Start generally, and move on to describe the finer points. You will find yourself naturally becoming more and more narrow and specific.

If flooded with impressions, maintain control and try not to respond immediately or try to get them all out at once. By not responding in such cases, you send a message to the subconscious to slow down.

You may also feel the impressions strongly, as if their source is in your own body. This is undesirable. If you find yourself being affected by the emotions of the object to where maintaining control is difficult, simply place the object down and break the contact. Wipe your hand with the washcloth.

Every psychometrist is a little different. With me, the insights, once started, come rapidly. I am often accused of being a speed-talker in these instances, but I give the information as quickly as I receive it. It is a stream-of-thought process you are trying to establish.

Sometimes the impressions flow rapidly. Other times, they come slowly. Do not worry if they are not there immediately. This is why describing the object is beneficial. It helps allay nervousness and panic over not having immediate impressions. They won't come immediately every time.

I give whatever I am impressed with, no matter how trivial or nonsensical it may seem to me. This is where many people get into trouble. They try to decipher everything they are impressed with while they are being impressed. They try to make sense of it all immediately. This will hinder the flow. Especially in the beginning. Give what you get as you get it.

There will come a time in which the two come together, but for the beginner, it is important to just establish the flow of impressions. Later, with the assistance of the object's owner, you will be able to filter through the information. The focus should be on whatever you may be impressed with.

As you develop this ability, the impressions you receive from the object will trigger psychic perceptions of other events surrounding the owner's life. This includes possible future events as well. The object sometimes provides insight into events and circumstances on the horizon.

Express these as well, but do so cautiously. Nothing is locked in stone. Events and situations can change. The individual should not be led to believe that events cannot be altered. Learn to develop ways of expressing this that help the individual to see new courses of action. Some of the techniques discussed in Chapter Seven will help with this.

Confirm your impressions: After doing the reading, I will hold the object up and ask for its owner to stand. At this point, I ask the owner how I did. For me, this is most important. Feedback establishes confidence.

It also helps build parameters for understanding your psychic impressions. If you felt something and it is confirmed, denied, or clarified for you in some way, then the next time you feel it or something similar, you will be in a better position to interpret it more accurately for the individual.

You will surprise yourself with how your accuracy improves with practice. Maybe, initially, you only hit two out of ten impressions, with some of the others being close. This is good. Twenty percent is usually considered higher than the law of chance.

Sample Psychometry Reading

This scenario is drawn from notes made following an actual psychometry reading I did for an individual about a year ago. She was single and in her mid-thirties. I had no other contact with this woman other than a brief conversation on the phone prior to her coming for an individual consultation. Although it was done in a one-on-one situation, I wrote it as if it were being done in a group situation. Usually, I begin such sessions with a brief discussion of what psychometry is and then move into a description of the object itself. The former I have left out of the following scenario:

I am holding in my hand a dainty, gold ring. It has on it two stones—a tiny emerald and a small diamond companion. It is very beautiful, and yet seems very fragile. This may in fact reflect the individual who is the owner. There is an understated beauty to her, and she probably feels that her heart is very fragile when it comes to intimate relationships. Having been hurt while very young in one serious relationship, there is a hesitancy to expose herself to that again. She probably feels her heart is fragile, but she also knows that when she gives her heart she gives it all.

This individual is looking for her prince. I don't feel that the ring is or was an engagement ring, but it caught her eye when she was younger—I'm feeling high school or first year of college with it—and it has been an important part of her make-up since.

The emerald is probably a symbol for her, it is probably her birth stone, but the diamond is the prince she wants to have as part of her life. The ring is the dream or wish that she holds near to her heart.

As I'm holding this ring, I am feeling an ache in my right knee. She probably has some stiffness there from a recent fall. It was down a long set of stairs—slipped on the carpet. The knee was hurt when she tried to stop. There is still a remnant of a bruise on her left hip.

This person has a great love of animals, almost an empathic response to them. Even stronger is her love of plants. She used to feel bad walking on and crushing grass. I hear her being teased about it.

As a side note, the unicorn was said to be so kind-hearted that it would walk so lightly that it would not even harm the grass beneath it. It is this same kind of energy I feel with this person. It would not surprise me to find that she has a love of unicorns.

I am also hearing in the background an old song ... "Get along home, Cindy, Cindy ...." There is a Cindy or Cynthia who is very important to the ring's owner .... This is a song from childhood, so it is probable that an old friend by this name has either recently or is going to come calling once more in your life.

Also I am picking up that there has been some squabbling with two family members. One is your mother, and the other is a family member that there has been much unspoken rivalry and competition with over the years.

On a final note, before I move on to someone else, I wish to return again to the idea of her prince, as reflected in the ring. When I first picked up the ring, the diamond stood out strongest, to me this suggests that a new prince either has or very soon—within three months time—will be riding into your life. Whether he is the one true prince for you, only time will tell, but he does have princely characteristics.

Afterwards, I requested feedback on what I had received from the ring, which she willingly provided. The ring was an engagement ring, but the marriage never came about. It was given to her the summer she graduated from high school. The emerald was her birthstone. Her heart had been broken so badly that she has been hesitant to commit fully in any relationship since.

She believes her heart to be too fragile to undergo similar experiences. She did keep the ring though, not as a momento of the lost marriage, but as a reminder to herself to keep her hopes for the ideal mate alive.

She had fallen about two weeks prior to her coming for the consultation, having slipped on the carpet at the top of a staircase. The knee was hurt, not when she tried to stop (as I had said), but when she did stop. It jammed into the wall. She did say that there were still remnants of the bruising she incurred bouncing down the stairs.

She takes in stray animals, and she said her house was like a miniature forest. She said that she hated seeing anything hurt, and as a child she would not step on bugs or walk through flowers. In response to my side note on unicorns, she laughed. She was a collector of them, and had 25 or 30 of them in her home.

As to the song "Cindy, Cindy," she could not place it at the time. Prior to writing this section, I contacted her, but it still was not something she found a connection to. She said there was a possibility, if it was interpreted a little differently, but I would not except that. (When it comes to psychometry and even most psychic information, it should either fit or not. I do not accept the idea of "making things fit.")

There had been some squabbling with her mother, but not another family member. She had said that she recently had an argument with her closest friend who was like a sister. She suggested that maybe that was what I meant. Again, I wouldn't accept that. It's too easy to force connections, and I see many psychics doing that inappropriately. You should never force the connections.

It is important to trust what first comes through and to hold to it. If you are having to force connections or give vague impressions that have multiple possible interpretations, then you are not honing your abilities appropriately. Initially this may occur, but with practice, you can become very specific. Learning to trust this is part of the development process. This is what psychometry helps to teach you.

Special Reminders

The psychometry experience is perfectly safe. The key is in learning to maintain control.

Training and practice are essential. It prevents inaccuracy and the misuse of the faculty.

Your own personality is beneficial to giving your impressions. Pay attention to your own reactions and responses as you touch and handle the object.

Remember, you are not an oracle. Although the development of psychometry can open up other psychic levels and insight into possible future occurrences, the key word is *possible*. Events and conditions can always be altered. There's a responsibility not to lead others into thinking otherwise.

Keep the development playful and joyful. It is easy to become discouraged. Avoid competition, even with probability charts. Some people/scientists work out intricate probability charts. These can be intimidating and may set a standard that does not apply to you. Any competition—with others in training, charts, or outsiders being read—will hinder relaxation. This in turn will block, hinder, or distort your impressions.

Don't allow negative emotions to clutter your mind while reading. Fear, anxiety, and doubt will create self-fulfilling situations. If it doesn't work (and there are times when it doesn't for everyone), avoid self-pity. Continue to practice.

Keep the development fun. Keep an open mind and don't force it. Relax, be cautiously optimistic, and you will succeed.

VI: Identifying personality

We have already discussed how easy it is for the imprint of people and/or events to magnetize objects. Some objects lend themselves well for psychometry, i.e. jewelry, letters, photos, etc. With most objects of single ownership, one of the easiest things to pick up on is the personality of the individual. The energy pattern of the person-ality is one of our strongest imprints.

In traditional spiritualism, a form of psy-chometry is used to connect with an individual for doing psychic readings and mediumship. It is called billets. A billet is simply a piece of paper that usually has the name and birthdate of the individual upon it. A name and birthdate are a person's two strongest energy signatures. They reflect much of the pattern of energies we have come into this life to develop and unfold. I usu-ally use billets when I do private consultation. By the individual signing his or her name, he/she places his/her energy into the paper. I then use it to do the initial attunement.

In this exercise you will be using billets. It is best performed with a development group or with friends. It is most important that you keep a light, playful attitude.

1. You will need small, equal-sized sheets of paper, one for each participant. Each must sign his/her name and birthdate upon it, and fold it at least twice. The name and birthdate must not be visible, and each participant should fold the paper the same number of times so there are no clues available as to who signed which papers.

2. After signing and folding the papers, each should hold it over the solar plexus area with both hands. Close your eyes and begin slow, deep, rhythmic breathing. Inhale for a count of four,

hold for a count of eight and then exhale for a count of four. See and feel yourself breathing your energy into the paper. Do this for several minutes.

3. After performing this, gather all of the billets into a bowl or hat and mix them up. Each person must then draw one out. Keep the paper folded and do not look at the name upon it.

4. In turn, each should describe some of the personality traits of the individual whose billet you hold. Keep it light and playful. This is just a warm-up exercise. Ask yourself some mental questions, and go only with your first thought or impression: Do your feel warm or cold?—Is this person reserved or open?—Is this person good-natured or serious?—What was the mood of this individual before meeting today?—What is the predominant emotion in this person's life at this time?

5. Keep the questions simple, and limit it to no more than four to six. There is no reason to write these down. This should be done only in a casual manner. Recording the responses may make some people feel pressured to perform.

6. Do not worry if you get your own. You shouldn't be able to read it or tell by the outside appearance. To further insure this, you may wish to have one individual do all of the folding of the billets. Getting your own can be very illuminating at times. Since you are treating it as if it is someone else's, there is a tendency to be objective. You

sometimes get a new perspective on yourself and where you are at.

VII: *Personal Touch*

This is another fun exercise, and should only be treated as such. This can be used in group settings—with those with whom you are familiar and even with strangers. It can be a wonderful warm-up for a group that is developing psychometry.

If done in a group setting, it should be done at the beginning. Any socializing and sharing of the day's activities among the participants will color the results, so you may wish to delay socializing until after the exercise.

1. Begin with a brief relaxation exercise.

2. Then pair off with someone you have not seen in the course of the day. Take a seat opposite him or her.

3. Hold hands with your partner. Close your eyes, and try to feel the other person's energy:

Does he or she feel warm or cold? (In this case, I am not referring to body temperature that may have been affected by weather conditions.) Is he/she relaxed? Has it been a fun day? Stressful? Successful? What is the general mood? Does a particular part of the body feel more stressed or tense? (Pay attention to what you feel in your own body.)

4. Trust whatever you feel. Even if you don't feel anything, trust whatever thought runs through your mind as you mentally ask yourself these questions. Such thoughts are often impressions that the subconscious is trying to communicate to you. Learning to recognize them and honor them by expressing them will amplify them in the future.

5. Share what you receive. Give each other feedback. Only through feedback about what you feel and are impressed with can you develop further confidence and clarity in your psychometry perceptions.

VIII: Image transference

Again, this is just a fun exercise. Although game-like, it can be used to develop and hone your psychometry skills. It can be done with just one other person.

1. Have a friend of yours hide an object that's important to you.

2. After having hidden it, have him/her sit down across from you. Take his/her hands in your own. Relax. You may even wish to breathe together. Synchronize your breathing. This helps establish harmony.

3. Throughout this, the individual who hid the object should form and hold a mental picture of where it is hidden.

4. As you hold the individual's hands, in a relaxed manner try to tune into his/her thoughts. This should *not* be strained or forced. Keep it light and relaxed. Allow a mental picture to form in your head.

5. Get feedback as to where it might be. Note anything that comes to mind. Even simple colors, although not a place, may reflect something near where it is located. Mention all that comes to your mind as you focus on your partner's thoughts.

Don't be discouraged if you are wrong. Keep it fun. Try this no more than four times at any one sitting or frustration can set it. This in turn will create blocks.

IX: *Symbolic perceptions*

Sometimes, the impressions you get may be vague and/or even symbolic. The subconscious mind will present to you feelings and images that should not be taken literally. They will need to be interpreted for the owner of the object from a symbolic perspective.

For example, you may be holding an object and feel an ache in your kidneys. This might indicate that the owner of the object has an actual health problem with the kidneys, but the ache or tingling in that area of your body may be symbolic. Since you know the kidneys serve to help filter the blood, maybe your attention is being drawn to the kidneys because the owner needs to start sifting and filtering what's going on in his/her life. Your response might be:

"As I am holding this ring, I am feeling a slight achiness in the area of the kidneys. This may indicate a problem with the kidneys, which may need to be checked by a physician, but it also may simply be symbolic. (It is okay to say that it might be symbolic.) Since the kidneys help to filter the blood, I may be feeling the achiness in my kidneys because the owner of this object needs to start using a little more discrimination and discernment. Filter through what's going on in your life. You don't have to accept everything …."

Remember to describe what you are feeling and what it probably indicates. Trust your instincts. Since you are receiving the impressions, it is your responsibility to translate them for the individual. Don't just say, "I feel an achiness in the kidneys, but it is probably symbolic rather than an actual physical problem." Your body is doing the attunement, so translate what you are feeling. Also keep in mind that such instances may be actual and symbolic at the same time.

How do you tell the difference between an actual and symbolic feeling? A lot of it is trial and error. It comes through practice. The more you practice and get feedback, the more criteria you have for determining whether an impression is actual or symbolic. It also requires that you understand and work more with symbology and the subconscious mind.

Symbology is the language of the subconscious. Since it mediates all energies coming into and going out of the body, it is beneficial to learn as much about it as possible. First, remember that the subconscious will only use images and symbols that it knows you can relate with and understand, if you put forth the effort.

Through the image of the symbol, the subconscious is able to make concrete the subtle ethereal perceptions it experiences. It serves as a bridge to understanding the perceptions we experience, but are not always conscious of.

To understand symbols is to understand ourselves. Each of us, at some point, will need to learn more about symbology and how to use it to our fullest capability. In working with symbols, start with your own perceptions and insights. Use free association. Can you relate it to something in your life?

Begin by asking yourself some simple questions: When I see this image, what do I usually relate it to? How does this image always make me feel? What does it mean to me? What do I associate with this symbol or image? Symbols and images touch both objective and subjective realities. They are a way in which the subconscious mind can bring forth information to the rational, conscious mind.

To help yourself with symbology, study the ones you use in your day-to-day life. This will provide greater insight into symbols that occur during psychometry perceptions. What is the significance behind the symbols in your church? Examine your surroundings, decor and furnishings. What do they say or symbolize about you? Look at your clothes, trinkets, jewelry and such. What do they say about you? What are they symbolizing about you and your attitudes?

Symbols are the language of the higher self. The interpretations will be individualistic initially, and it will change as you grow, learn, and develop. With psychometry though, the spontaneous interpretation is important, but keep in mind that it is just the start.

X: Using psychometry

There are many ways of using psychometry. A keepsake from a loved one who has passed on can be a means of keeping in touch with the shared love and experiences. Using psychometry with rocks, crystals and minerals can be a means of keeping in touch with nature. Even plants and flowers can be used for this. A technique of flower clairsentience will be discussed later in this book.

Pictures and photos are a powerful means of connecting with the life currents of those depicted.

How often have we picked up an old photo of a distant friend and then become flooded with a variety of emotions. Then to top it off, within a couple of hours we receive a phone call from our friend. Photos are links to those within them. Through psychometry we can attune to them.

Although it doesn't directly apply to psychometry, it is important to note that one of the first things I usually teach in classes on psychic self-defense is that all possessions and especially photos, are doorways/links to you. When a relationship ends, you should try to take back all photos and personal items. The average individual wouldn't know how to use them, but they can be a direct way of staying connected. They carry your imprints. Someone trained can use them to attune to you regularly and even send messages and feelings to you.

Initially, when you start to practice psychometry, work with a variety of objects and materials. You will find that some are easier for you to work with than others. One person may find cloth easier, while another finds that jewelry works best. We are each unique, and must develop along the lines easiest and best for us. Also, by working with a variety of materials, you develop greater flexibility in your skills. You may not always have access to something cloth or metal.

Practice psychometrizing regularly, but do so at different times. Some individuals find they are more psychic at night, while others are during the day. We each have our own cycles. By adjusting and practicing at different times, we learn greater control over our perceptive abilities. We learn to use it at will.

You do not have to develop this ability in a group. You can work on it alone. There are some drawbacks to this, the most obvious being that you cannot get the instant feedback which develops confidence in your abilities. It also eliminates being hindered by competition with others, whether tangible or not.

If you do practice alone, keep a record of your impressions, just as you would with a group. Tape record them or write them down as you touch and hold the object. Keep track of dates and such. Go to second-hand stores and thrift shops and handle objects. How do they make you feel? Buy some trinkets, old books and even inexpensive articles of clothing. Psychometrize them. What kinds of feelings do you get about their previous owners and their lives? Occasionally pick up a pen of a fellow worker or friend, and through it get an idea as to how they are feeling. Then, in casual conversation you can get your feedback.

I don't recommend doing this often to friends and co-workers without their permission, as there are ethical laws of privacy. We do not really have the right to tune into other people's private lives without their permission. It can be done, but there is an ethics involved. I know a lot of psychics who will tune into anyone anytime they are asked, which I feel is inappropriate.

On more than a few occasions, I have had individuals come to me to tune into relatives and friends. They pull out photos of in-laws, nieces, nephews, neighbors, etc., and they want to know who is fooling around on whom, who is cheating, or a myriad of other trivial things that have nothing to do with the individual's own life, other than to provide fodder for gossip.

I tell people straight out, that I do not tune into others without their permission. Tuning into someone without their permission can be like opening their mail. We wouldn't want someone going through our mail, so we shouldn't go through theirs. On the other hand we all tune into others to some degree; it is part of the self-preservation instinct. We assess people and situations to determine degrees of comfort or discomfort we are likely to encounter. Not to do so and honor those perceptions can be foolish, and most people have gotten away from that. Psychometry helps us relearn that ability.

The only exceptions that I make are for family members who are not adults, i.e. children and such, still living at home. I also will tune into things if it concerns health issues. These are my personal ethics. They are my choices. I do not like nor tolerate people intruding or nosing into my life, so I honor that in others. The greater your ability, the greater your responsibility.

❦❧

❧ 4 ❧

Enhancing Your
Sense of Touch

We are exposed to a wide variety of energies and
perceptions throughout the day—sound, sights,
electricity, and other fields. Most either go unrec-
ognized, or are brushed aside. One of the marvelous capabilities of the subconscious mind is its
ability to mediate and process all those energies
and subtle perceptions. It is sensitive to all sensory information and data that we encounter and
interact with in the course of the day.

We are not always consciously aware of this
sensory stimuli and interplay with our own bodies. Much of it passes through us, like a breeze
that comes through an open window. The subconscious mind is aware of it all, even though the
conscious mind is not. The subconscious mind
filters through it all and determines what is significant and what isn't. It picks up subtle signs
and innuendoes in speech and posture. It hears
undertones in vocalizations. It can detect and
reflect imprints of people, places, and things—
past and present.

Ideally, we should be able to shift gears and access that bank of information and perception that we call the subconscious mind at any time. We can develop and train ourselves to do this—to be more sensitive and conscious to all we experience. We can even learn to be selectively conscious of subtle impressions. It requires focus and learning to use altered states of consciousness.

There are many states of consciousness. We have a work consciousness, a play consciousness, a romantic consciousness, etc. We slip into various modes of consciousness frequently throughout the day, according to our need and/or circumstances. Daydreaming is an altered state, as is night dreaming. Absent-mindedness reflects an altered state of consciousness. As a child, when you were spinning around until you became dizzy, you were inducing an altered state of consciousness. Trance, hypnosis, and meditation are means of altering consciousness. So are drugs and alcohol, but they should be avoided in developing your psychic sensibilities.

For our purposes, we will define an altered state of consciousness as any state of being which is different from our normal, ordinary, rational state of mind. It is a relaxed state of mind and body. It is a state other than that which you use as you go about your day-to-day business.

Whenever you become absorbed in anything, you often slip into an altered state. You are usu-

Conscious	Sense Perception
	Expression Rational Mind
	Day-to-Day Activities
	10% of Body & Brain Controlled

⬆⬆⬆
⬇⬇⬇

Sub-conscious	Autonomic Nervous System Registers all Perceptions
	Creativity Intuition
	Higher Sense Perception 90% of Body & Brain Function Controlled

The Conscious and Subconscious Minds

With psychometry we hold and handle an object to access any energy imprints left upon it by the owner. The subconscious perceives these, but we must access the subconscious to read them.

ally very relaxed and oblivious to things going on outside of you. Artists and creative people learn to use altered states consciously. They develop a high degree of focus and concentration. Conscientious practice with the exercises in this book will help you to develop control of altered states, particularly in their application to psychometry.

Aids to Psychic Touch

It takes practice to train the mind and the body to work together consciously. The exercises in this chapter (and all of the others) are designed to assist you in this. They will not automatically work for you. Don't be afraid to adapt them. They are drawn from a variety of sources and individuals who have achieved some degree of success in shifting consciousness to read vibrations and imprints. They will help you enhance your overall perceptive and intuitive abilities in general. Specifically, they will help you enhance your psychic touch faculty.

There will be off days. Sometimes you will find it difficult to achieve an altered state. Some exercises will be more successful for you than others. Some will be more difficult. Sometimes the responses will be slow, so be careful about giving up too quickly.

Persistence is the key. Try to keep a set time for concentrated practice and development. Other opportunities that arise throughout the day or week will then just further hone what you are developing. With practice, everyone will achieve some success after just a few attempts. It will be enough to encourage your further development.

Keep your practice short. Try an exercise several times, and if it is not succeeding, move on to another one. It may simply be that the exercise is not a good criteria for you to determine your success. Staying too long with any one exercise creates frustration and doubt. And remember that doubts are damaging. If you run into a block, move on to some other exercise or try another day.

EXERCISES

XI: *Beginning preparations*

Attitude is most important. Expect success. Keep in mind that you are learning something new. When you first began to read, you had to learn the alphabet and develop a vocabulary. The development of psychometry is the same thing.

Put your mind in order. Clear out the rubbish of the day. Take some time to just relax. The more relaxed you are the easier it is to access the subconscious mind.

Don't eat within one hour of the scheduled time to practice psychometry—at least six hours if you are eating heavy. The lighter you are, the more energy you will have to attune. It takes more energy for digestion than any other bodily function. If you haven't been eating, then the subconscious is entirely free to focus on what you wish it to.

Wash or wipe your hands before handling objects to be psychometrized. This cleanses them of residue of previously handled objects.

Some individuals prefer to perform psychometry with wet hands. It is very raccoon-like. Raccoons have had a reputation for ages of washing their food before they eat it. In reality, they are wetting their hands to increase the sensitivity of them and facilitate handling the food. Experiment with this.

Water does help stimulate sensitivity of the hands and the chakras within it. It is a good conductor of electricity, and this facilitates receiving the impressions imprinted on the object. At the very least, you should have a wet cloth to work with.

XII: Touch

Some oils and fragrances are beneficial for stimulating the chakras in the hands and fingers, making them more sensitive to what they touch. They also stimulate altered states of consciousness, and this makes it easier to access the subconscious. Most essential oils are very strong, and all that is required is that a drop be used either in a small bowl of water or in the palm of the hand itself. Again, experiment. The following oils are generally beneficial for use in psychometry:

- Eucalyptus oil—This strong healing oil has wonderful applications for enhancing psychometry abilities. It penetrates and calms, making perceptions more distinct and clear. It also helps to prevent you from becoming emotionally connected to the impressions you receive through the object. Dabbing it in the area of the third eye (brow) will facilitate shifting into psychic perceptions. It activates the brow chakra center. There is usually a warm sensation. (If too warm, dilute with water.) This is especially effective when reading imprints by holding the object(s) against the forehead. Massaging it into the palm of the hand and the tips of the fingers will activate these energy centers as well. When they are stimulated it is easier to sense through the hands and/or fingers. This can be used not only for psychometry but also for various forms of healing through touch.

- Gardenia—Gardenia is a very protective oil and fragrance stabilizing to the emotions. It is a fragrant oil that I often recommend for those working in the mental health field. It prevents them from becoming attached to the issues and emotions, and helps the individual maintain objective distancing. I have found it to be useful in several ways for those beginning to develop psychic touch. One of the problems sometimes encountered in developing psychometry skills is that the individual begins to "connect" to everyone and everything he/she touches. This most often occurs with individuals who have a natural propensity for empathic responses. This will be explored more fully in Chapter Six. It can be beneficial to soak the cleansing washcloth in water that has gardenia oil in it. This prevents any lingering emotional residue from the object affecting the psychometrist. Another trick is to have a bowl of water with gardenia oil within it. Dip your hands into it before each reading of an object. This helps you to read the object without becoming emotionally affected by the impressions received.

- Honeysuckle—This fragrance is what was once known as an "attraction oil." It sharpens the intuition. By anointing the palm of the hand with it, it enhances your ability to read others with whom you shake hands. More importantly, dabbing it under the eyes and on the brow will enhance the sensitivity of the face. This is especially effective for those who find it easier to pick up impressions through facial contact rather than through hand. Making a facial wash with honeysuckle oil is beneficial for those who psychometrize through the cheeks and forehead. Add a drop of oil to a mixing bowl of water and stir. Using your clean hands, softly splash the mixture over the face. You may wish to allow it to air dry or you may wish to dab it dry. You do not need to do this between every reading. The effects of the wash last.

- Sage—Sage is a general, all-purpose oil with many wonderful properties. It cleanses, protects, and stimulates higher sensibilities. Spiritual inspirations and perceptions are brought forth more clearly to the conscious mind. It is also beneficial for stimulating appropriate ways of expressing your impressions. In psychometry, it is especially beneficial for those who would read objects through the solar plexus. Simply anoint the solar plexus area with a drop or two of oil. Lay or hold the object next to this area. (It does not have to be done through the skin. Impressions will be received through clothing.)

Remember that most true essential oils are potent, and they can be irritating to the skin. Dilute them, rather than use them directly on the skin surface.

XIII: Activating the hands

In Chapter Two we briefly mentioned the human chakra system. One way of looking at it is by seeing the chakras as outreaches of the subconscious mind. The subconscious mind has many levels. Different levels of the subconscious control different physiological functions and other energy expressions of the body, mind and spirit.

For example, the solar plexus chakra is tied to that level of the subconscious mind which controls digestion, the body's assimilation of nutrients and even left brain activity. This level of the subconscious mind also mediates empathic and feeling responses and clairsentient abilities.

Although the subconscious is mind activity, it will reflect itself most strongly through specific points of the body. These points are where there is a greater degree of electro-magnetic emanations. Massaging, or in other ways stimulating, those points of the body are means of activating specific levels of the subconscious mind.[9]

In the palms of the hands and at the tips of the fingers are chakras or energy centers. Meridians and energy pathways also circulate throughout the body. Most of the major meridians of the

9 To further understand the role of the chakras and their connections to the subconscious, along with ways to stimulate and activate them more effectively, consult my earlier work: *The Healer's Manual: A Beginner's Guide to Vibrational Therapies*, Llewellyn Publications

body terminate at the tips of the fingers. Because of this, the hands can be used to sense and/or project subtle energy.

Periodically, when I do aura analysis for people, I will encounter individuals who have soft spirals of energy emanating from the tips of the fingers. Sometimes the entire hand is encircled with vibrant energy. I encounter this most often among massage practitioners, physical therapists, nurses, practicing artists and those who are using their hands regularly in some kind of creative or healing process.

By stimulating and activating these chakra centers, we make ourselves more receptive to impressions upon objects. It is easier to feel the energy imprints of the owner of the object.

The simplest and fastest way of activating the chakras in the palms of the hands is simply by rubbing the hands together. Rub them briskly for 15 to 30 seconds. To activate the chakras at the tips of the fingers, simply bring the tips of each hand together and rub them together. For the finger tips, you may wish to do this for a minute or so. (Rubbing the tips of the fingers together also stimulates all of the meridians/energy pathways of the body. This is very healthful and balancing to the body.)

This rubbing will increase the sensitivity. You may remember some old movies in which bank robbers and safe crackers would rub the tips of their fingers against the palm of one hand or even against sandpaper before trying the combination. It stimulated and heightened their sense of touch. With this exercise you are heightening your sense of touch to unlock the imprints of an object.

To test whether the chakras have been activated, extend your hands in front of you after having rubbed them briskly together. Hold them about a foot apart. Slowly bring the palms together. Bring them as close as you can without them touching. Then draw them apart to about six inches, and then repeat this in and out movement. Keep the movements slow and steady.

As you perform this testing, pay attention to what you feel or sense. You may feel warmth or coolness. You may experience a feeling of pressure building up. It will seem as if the space is thickening between the hands. You are just more able to sense the space than before.

Experiment with this stimulation:

1. Shuffle an ordinary deck of playing cards.
2. Rub your hands briskly together.
3. Draw the first card off the top, and hold it face down between the palms of your hands.
4. Take a deep breath, relax and try to feel if it is a black card or a red. Go with your first impression. Keep in mind that one out of five is chance; more than that has moved you into some other realm.

Chakras in the hands

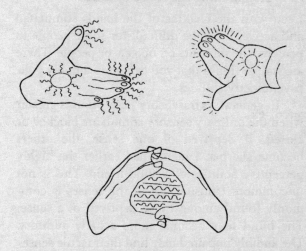

5. If you get good at this, place the card in a shoe-box. Hold the box and try to determine its color.

This activating through brisk rubbing should be done before any psychometry reading. It will enhance your overall sensitivity and your accuracy through touch. It will enable you to experience the energy imprints of objects and people more clearly.

XIV: Heightening the sense of touch

Even with the chakras of the hands stimulated and active, it can be difficult for some people to perceive the imprints on objects or people. There are simple things that you can do to amplify your psychometry abilities.

In general, extrasensory perception is greater when the ordinary sensory stimuli are blocked or closed. If deprived of one sense, the others become sharper. I mentioned earlier the highly perceptive abilities of a blind friend. This is not uncommon. Unusual use of the senses is commonly found among those deprived of a sense. The blind may become more acutely auditory. The audibly impaired may find their tactile senses heightened.

We can mimic this, and fool the body into shifting into higher sensory perceptions. Many psychics and clairvoyants will "read" a person or an object with their eyes closed. I do this myself. For me, it heightens the responses I receive on other levels, and it also prevents me from using the client's own responses as clue to the kind of psychic information and its direction. I am less likely to key off of their body language and/or facial expressions.

Try the card reading experiment in the previous exercise with your eyes closed or blindfolded. Compare the results of this with the original

Activating the hand chakras

The in and out movement of the hands activates the chakras in their palms. This makes them more sensitive to touch, making the space between them and even objects held within them more perceptible.

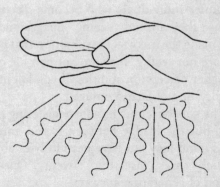

With practice, you can develop a sensitivity and control that can eliminate the need to hold the object. Just holding your hand over it will enable you to sense.

results. Place some cotton plugs in your ears and wear a blindfold as well while performing the card experiment. Again compare your results. Then move on to other objects. You will find that at the very least, psychometrizing objects with eyes closed will eliminate visual distractions and enhance your concentration.

XV: Twenty questions

Everyone will experience the psychometry perceptions a little differently. Some may have vague, undefined feelings, while others may have detailed scenarios pass through their minds. Your way of perceiving is no better and no worse than anyone else's. It is simply yours.

When teaching development, I often encounter individuals who become discouraged because they are not "seeing" images and such. They make the incorrect assumption that because they are not seeing, they are not psychic or have no higher perception abilities. If you fall into this category, do not be discouraged.

The subconscious mind is registering perceptions, but the bridge between it and your conscious mind may not have been fully established. In such cases, use the "Twenty Questions" method of generating answers.

1. Begin by performing a relaxation exercise.
2. Rub the hands together to activate the chakras.

3. Take the object to be psychometrized in your hand.

4. Examine it closely, and then close your eyes.

5. Move it around in your hands. Run your fingers over it. Place it against the solar plexus or forehead.

6. Do not worry if no images or impressions come to mind. They may just be slow, or they may be registering in other ways. This is where the questioning comes in. Mentally ask yourself simple questions of the object and its owner. Keep them simple and uncomplicated. Framing them for "Yes" or "No" responses is effective. Trust what comes to mind. Some sample questions follow: Is the owner male or female? Is this person generally upbeat or down? What is the general disposition of this person? Is there an issue prominent in this person's life? Is it family? Business? Personal? Is there a color significant to this person? (Remember that you may not see the color, but you may think or feel yellow, for example. Give what you think at the time.) Is there something special about this object? Unique? Significant to its owner? Is there a person who is important to the object's owner at this time? If so, is there a name? An initial?

7. These kinds of questions are essential to ask. Remember that you may not see or hear the answer. You may only think it. For example, if

there were a color important to the person, what do you think it would be? Then give what comes to mind. Give your first impressions. Don't hesitate or try to explain them initially. As you develop your skills, you will find that you are more capable of doing this. Initially, it is simply important to build that bridge between the subconscious and the conscious. As you start to speak what you think or are impressed with, the bridge builds stronger and firmer. The answers become more clear.

8. Speak your answers and impressions with confidence. When using the questioning method of generating insights, phrase your answers in a way that includes the question. For example, if you mentally ask about a color, and blue comes to mind, simply say, "I see (feel, am impressed with...) the color blue. To me this would indicate _____ about this person and/or object."

9. Remember, sometimes all it takes is to speak out loud what you are impressed with for the doors to open wide. By speaking your impressions, thoughts, images, etc. about the object, you draw from the subconscious to the conscious. You are taking the impressions out of that ethereal mental realm of the subconscious mind and grounding them into physical expression.

10. It is often with the speaking of impressions that the meaning of them to the individual

becomes clear. Oftentimes, our dreams do not make sense until we speak of them or record them. Then the lights go on. With psychometry, the describing of the object and any impressions will help do the same thing. It stimulates understanding and clarification.

❦

❧ 5 ❧

Furthering Your Development

Psychometry is one of the easiest psychic abilities to develop. There are many applications for it. It can be used to assess people and your potential compatibility with them. It can be used to locate lost items and missing persons. It can be used to detect and explore energy imbalances within the body, mind, and spirit. Some of these will be explored within this chapter, and some of them will be explored later throughout the book.

Psychometry is a psychic faculty that enables you to gain confirmation of your impressions more easily than with other methods. Its development teaches you to honor your feelings on all levels.

As with any psychic ability, though, there are things to keep in mind in its development. Its development does not make you qualified to be a professional psychic counselor anymore than having a driver's license makes you a professional race car driver. This chapter is for those who may want to hone their skills and maybe begin to explore the possibilities of using them to help others. At the end of the chapter are more complex exercises for taking your awakening abilities even further. The following precautionary notes will help you in developing your higher sensibilities for this purpose. These are even further elaborated upon in Chapter Seven.

Develop the proper attitude: Your own personal attitude toward the realities of psychic energy and higher consciousness plays a critical role. Blocks that inhibit your full acceptance can sometimes be subtle.

Psychic ability is not a peculiar gift bestowed by nature or the Divine upon certain specially gifted individuals. It is a natural ability, innate within every living human. No one is more or less gifted than anyone else. Be wary of those who profess such. It is the same as developing any skill. It requires exercise, practice, and persistence.

"Nothing in the world can take the place of persistence. Talent will not; nothing is more common than unsuccessful men with talent. Genius will not; unrewarded genius is almost a proverb. Education will not; the world is full of educated derelicts. Persistence and determination are omnipotent."[10]

It is the attitude of the individual that is most crucial. Learning as much about the human mind

---

10 Regardie, Israel. *The Complete Golden Dawn System of Magic*. Falcon Press; Phoenix, Arizona, 1984.

and consciousness is important to the development and balanced expression of psychic abilities within your life. More than this though is believing you can develop it. What you think, you become. Change your imaginings and you can change the world.

Any legitimate and qualified psychic is one who took time to develop, unfold, stabilize and maintain control of his or her psychic energies. This requires discipline. It requires time, and it requires practice. The faculty must be trained just as with any other faculty of the mind or ability of the body.

Don't buy into old myths about the psychic realm: There are many old myths about psychic development that inhibit or block personal unfoldment. It is important to be able to recognize them and move past them. In most cases, it simply requires that you examine it from a common sense perspective.

One of the subtlest influences of our ability or inability to develop psychic potential is our religious or spiritual perception. For many, anything dealing with the psychic has reflections of evil. On the other hand, many believe that only a truly spiritual person is one who can truly develop this ability.

Neither of these perceptions is true. Psychic faculties are not supernatural. Unfortunately, many people approach its development as a reflection of spirituality or something supernatural. This kind of perception creates hero worship and places others on pedestals. Or if you are the psychic, it places you on a pedestal that you will not be able to live up to.

Psychic energy is neutral. It is neither good nor evil in itself. The ability is inherent within us all. It is only how we use and express the ability that determines its level of goodness or evil. Morality and spirituality do not necessarily go hand in hand with psychic ability. A person who is physically strong is not necessarily evil nor good. If that strength is expressed through bullying and negative aggression, then we can determine its degree of "evilness." The same is true of psychic expression.

Another myth is that you must have developed it in a past life to be truly good with it in this life. I often hear individuals in the field professing that they are gifted because of past lives.

These kinds of statements should trigger strong warning bells. Regardless of any degree of development in a past life, the qualities and abilities must still be awakened, developed, and expressed anew within this life. Yes, there may be an occasional prodigy, but most of us will have little contact with them, and even their abilities must be re-schooled and controlled. If we learned to read in a past life, we still have to learn to read again within the present. The same applies to psychic development.

Usually, those who proclaim their gifts based upon previous lives are trying to make themselves out as something unique and specially gifted. The same goes for those who give credit for their abilities based upon some physical accident, as is often depicted in books and movies. Again, this makes them appear us unusual. It implies that their abilities are out of the ordinary, something that an average individual is unable to develop.

Although there are rare instances of such, we should be wary of those proclaiming it. In such cases it is almost always atavistic in nature. The individual usually is able to control neither the intensity of the experience nor the time and means of its expression.

Trauma that triggers spontaneous expressions of psychic energies will affect the person on other levels of their being as well. Although it may not reflect this immediately, usually within three to seven years it does. And it never qualifies the individual to provide counseling or to set themselves up as an authority.

Control of your abilities is essential: In the development of psychometry, or any psychic ability, there should always be control. Control comes through developing focused attention and concentration. Ideally, we should be able to turn our psychic abilities on and off at will. We must also be able to apply directed observation and attention to the impressions we receive. A good psychic is neither a "dreamy, space cadet" nor impractical. This kind of concentrated focus is necessary to be successful in any area of life.

Psychic information, such as that derived through psychometry, must be processed quickly. It must be recorded in the conscious mind and passed on. This means that the conscious mind must select and apply discernment of the impressions. They must be placed in a sequence that will be comprehensible to the individual.

Now most of us do have some blind spots, but through trained observation, many of them can be eliminated or diminished. All impressions must be realized, recorded, and translated for the individual. If this is not done quickly—if not immediately—it becomes mixed with all of your other brain stuff which will distort it. (This is also why it is usually best to go with first impressions.) The ability to do all this requires great control, and only comes through practice.

Even if your intuitive information is good, the presentation of it should be strong and balanced. Jumbled fragments, rather than a coherent series of statements, will only confuse the client. Psychic information often comes in blocks of knowledge. You may have a psychological bias toward the information which will color your presentation of it. An imperfect discernment and selection of the intuitive information is usually due to a lack of mental and intuitive control.

Construct a proper code of behavior for using your abilities: This code of behavior, its proper expression and application in every day life is an essential part of control. Many psychics believe it is all right to tune into others without their permission. In many ways this is like opening another person's mail without his/her permission. It is an uncontrolled use. It is disrespectful to the other person.

I personally have a problem with those who do so, as I am a firm believer in honoring the Law of Privacy. I resent others trying to intrude into my private life, and so I am very careful not to do it with others. Even if I do pick up on some things, I usually will never let on. First, it can make others nervous around you, and furthermore, you need to be sure how the individual will respond to the information before giving it.

There are exceptions, of course. Regarding health and safety issues, I will forego this. I am very aware of possible repercussions, and it is a fully conscious decision on my part to do so. If it works out—wonderful. If it doesn't, I am willing to suffer the consequences of my actions.

In all such cases, I am careful to present the information in a non-threatening manner. This is part of control. Psychic information and impressions should be presented in a manner that is beneficial and uplifting. Even negative impressions can be presented to the individual in ways that reveal hidden possibilities for growth.

To be able to do so, you need to have some basic skills and formal and legitimate training in counseling techniques. This should be a basic requirement for anyone setting themselves up as a public psychic counselor. It is too easy to inadvertently influence an individual in an inappropriate manner.

When a client comes to you for any psychic information—whether through psychometry or through any other means, you should be prepared for all possibilities. In psychic readings and consultations, and even in teaching situations, the clients are placing themselves in a receptive and often vulnerable position. Because of this, they are more easily influenced by what you say, so great caution and preparation is necessary.

Get some formal training in counseling: Audit some college courses. Volunteer on hot lines. Attend some night classes. They won't necessarily make you a competent therapist or counselor, but they will provide practical techniques for handling certain situations and communicating effectively with different kinds of people. Several of these are provided for you in Chapter Seven.

Most people that come to psychics can be placed into one of two categories. They either are looking for quick, effortless solutions—which include allowing the psychic to tell them how best to live their lives—or they are looking for intuitive and creative guidance and parameters for handling their life situations. They are looking for some possible directions. In either case, counseling training is beneficial and will make you more effective in helping people empower themselves.

Most psychic work revolves around three issues: health, money/jobs, and love. Many people come to psychics looking for easy answers and solutions. Life does not work that way. Often what people need is not psychic information, but some common sense, a new perspective or insight that reveals more creative options for them. It is not the psychic counselor's role to direct the lives of their clients. It is not the psychic's role to tell the individual what to do. The psychic should help the individual take greater control over his or her own life path.

The psychic counselor should provide insight and options. He or she should show what is likely to occur if certain courses of action are taken. In this way the individual is able to make his or her own decision. The responsibility for his or her life is placed within the hands of the individual. It is ultimately healing and more empowering for the individual.

Many come with serious problems and issues. Providing psychic information at such times rather than helping them more fully does them a disservice. It often keeps the individual dependent upon the psychic.

Several years ago, I was at a metaphysical expo in which I was a featured speaker. I was also doing mini-psychic readings as part of the promotion. My first two readings on the second day of this expo were intense. The first lady was in the midst of a great crisis in her life and was very suicidal. The second was with a woman whose husband of only one year had left her because his ex-wife had died recently and he blamed himself and his new wife.

Obviously, in fifteen minutes time, there is no way to resolve these situations—nor should the attempt be made. It is also not a time to present psychic information. Both individuals needed to speak with qualified therapists. My efforts went toward trying to calm them and to direct them to agencies or individuals who were in a better position to help them.

These are not unusual situations to encounter. This is why training in crisis counseling is essential for any professional psychic. One of the things I often do when I go into a new area is go through the phone book and write the numbers down for social service agencies to cover all possibilities.

Your intuitive impression may develop strongly, but you must also know how to present the information in a manner the client can use. Keep in mind that most coming to you are coming because of real problems—not necessarily for psychic impressions. Counseling and the psychic must go hand in hand.

Special Reminders

You will have times in which you are more effective than others. Note them as you practice the exercises in this book. Do they correspond to certain phases of the moon? Certain times of the day?

Make sure you are physically comfortable when you work. If you are uncomfortable, it will be more difficult to concentrate.

Don't try to give meaning to everything immediately. Begin by describing your impressions and move on. The meaning will clarify itself as you speak.

Don't ask too many questions of the individual. They have come to you for answers. Too many questions will not only make them doubtful of your abilities, but it sends a message to the subconscious that you are unsure.

Always close down the session clearly. This is especially important if you are at all uncomfortable or the impressions are too intense.

Set up your own ritual, something physical that you do, which reflects this closing down. Return the object to the owner. Then send a mental message to your subconscious, willing it to close down. Wipe your hands with the cloth. Involve yourself with some physical activity. Eat something light. The subconscious and the body's energies become focused on digestion. It is very grounding.

A Good Psychic Is...

- A good psychic counselor is able to attune to the person and/or situation.
- A good psychic counselor is one who will, at the same time of tuning in, be able to perceive how the individual will respond to the information. This information can then be expressed in a non-threatening, productive, and more receptive manner.
- A good psychic counselor will always express the information in a manner that will be understood by the individual.
- A good psychic counselor will provide insight, new possibilities and beneficial options or courses of action in regards to the situation.
- A good psychic counselor will do all of this without intruding upon the free will of the client.

EXERCISES

XVI: *Enhancing concentration and focus*

One of the most difficult faculties for many to develop is concentration and focus. There are so many distractions within our busy lives, that our mind often seems scattered. By developing focused attention, you become more successful in all aspects of life—not just the psychic.

Concentration is the art of holding the image that you have created or allowed to surface within your mind without the mind wavering or wandering to other things. You should be able to develop concentrated focus that is strong enough to hold one image to the exclusion of all others.

Exercises such as what follows can be practiced regularly and will help develop and strengthen this ability in you. Begin by performing a progressive relaxation. The more relaxed you are, the easier it is to concentrate.

1. Close your eyes and create a mental picture. The picture should be as clear as something in the physical. Make it as life-like as possible. Give it color, fragrance, texture—all the physical qualities it would have in real life.

A simple exercise is to visualize an orange. See its shape, size, and color in your mind. Feel the skin on it. What does it feel like as you press your finger into it and begin to peel it? Notice the fragrance as the juice squirts out. Then in your mind create also the image and experience of its taste.

Then try this with other fruits and objects. Each has its own unique experience, and it will force the mind to concentrate. It only takes several minutes to perform such exercises, and they are very beneficial for stimulating the subconscious and your ability to focus it. This strengthens your concentration.

Decide to hold it steady within the mind for a reasonable time. Start by trying to do so for three minutes. If you find that this is too difficult, cut back the time. If it is too easy, regularly increase the length of time.

As you get better at this, you may want to try and do this in different locations and with the eyes open. Begin where there are no distractions. Then try to focus solely on the image when there are others present. Try theaters, while waiting in lines, during lunch. As you work on this you will find that you can apply concentrated focus with greater ease and with less distractions in most environments.

2. Another simple but progressively effective exercise for developing focused concentration is through counting. It is an exercise I frequently use when I teach development classes. As always begin by relaxing and closing the eyes. Initially, you may want to have someone else do the counting, or you can do it yourself.

Slowly count to 10. Focus exclusively on each number until the next is sounded. Try and visualize it in your mind. Sound it in your mind. Focus only on the number.

If you are part of a meditation or development group, alternate individuals counting to 10 or 20. When you or someone else in the group is doing the counting, vary the rhythm. Count irregularly with varied rhythms and speeds. By doing so, you avoid anticipation in the switching of focus, and concentration is enhanced.

Pay attention to your own thought processes as the counting occurs. Does your mind wander? If such thoughts as, "Oh, this isn't so difficult," occurs, then you need to work on your concentration. You should eventually be able to count to 100 with little or no distraction or mind-wandering.

XVII: Increasing the sensitivity of your hands

Hands and fingers are our tools for touching, caressing, and handling life's experiences. We use them to give and to take, to attract and repel, to grasp or to push away. They can be raised in benediction or in anger. In traditional symbolism, the position of the hand was what was significant. Each finger had its meaning, personal and astrological. Our hands are wonderful instruments. Through them we can touch others and channel the love within our hearts. Through them we hold onto others within our life. Through them also we learn to release what we know is no longer beneficial.

There are a lot of ways of increasing the overall sensitivity of the hands. One of the most practical and easiest is through massage and reflexology.

Within the hands are points that are connected to every part of the body. Oriental medicine teaches the existence of meridians or energy pathways. Most of the primary meridians terminate at the fingertips. Thus by massaging and working with the fingertips alone, we are able to stimulate the major energy patterns of the body. This can be used for improving health and for increasing psychic sensitivities.

Reflexology is the theory that a certain part of the body is a reflection or a map to the entire body. In Chinese medicine, the hands, feet and ears are dynamic reflexology points—they have links to every part of the body. A sore spot on the hand or foot will usually indicate a problem in some other area of the body.

Reflexology is the use of acupressure or massage on certain parts of the hands to stimulate other parts of the body. This kind of massage is a dynamic tool for stress reduction and the relief of pain. For example, by massaging a tender spot on the hand, you relieve or even heal a problem with an internal organ.

This work can in no way explore the complete intricacies of reflexology and Chinese medicine. There are many books currently available on the subject. You may even wish to consult my book, *The Healer's Manual*, which has a good introduction to the major meridians of the body.

Do simple massages upon the hands on a regular basis. You can have someone do it for you or you can use one hand to massage the other. You may even choose to use an oil or lotion scented with fragrances that enhance psychometry. The following method is simple and will enhance overall sensitivity of touch.

1. Use the thumb in a creeping motion or with a slight pinching and rolling motion to massage the entire palm surface. Working from the wrist toward the fingers. Keep the pressure comfortable. The idea is to stimulate without hurting.

2. Using your thumb and first finger in a pinching motion, massage each finger individually. Give special attention to joints, the tips and the area around the fingernail.

3. Go to the back of the hand. Work in a line from the fingers to just below the wrist. Follow the hollows between the bones.

XVIII: Feeling group energy

This exercise is not only fun but also beneficial. It is most effective when used with compatible groups. It teaches that the hands are not only receptive to energy, but can be used to direct and send it as well.

There are many variations of this exercise possible, so do not be afraid to experiment. It is easiest to begin with simply trying to identify the object charged with the energy of the group.

1. Have four or five objects, they can be different or the same. If the same, there should be a way of distinguishing one from the others. Using four or five differently colored balls is helpful.

2. Each person will take a turn at sensing. The sensor should be separated from the group while the charging of the object is performed by the group.

3. The group chooses one of the objects and separates it from the others. The idea is to charge it with pure energy, so that it can be felt more strongly than the other objects.

4. There are several ways of charging it. One is to have each individual take the singled out object and hold it in his/her lap. Close the eyes and begin rhythmic breathing. Inhale for a count of four, hold for a count of four and exhale for a count of four.

With each inhalation, visualize pure crystalline energy drawing down through the head and as you exhale, visualize it streaming forth from your hands and your body to permeate the object. See and feel the object charging with dynamic energy.

This can also be performed as a group. Simply place the object in the midst of the group, and pump energy into it in unison. Do this for several minutes.

5. Place the object in the midst of the others.

6. The group member who is out of the room, is invited back in. He or she must then feel which object has been charged. This can be done by holding each object in turn or even by simply holding the hands over the objects to sense and determine which has the higher charge.

Monitor what you feel with each object. Pay attention to sensations in the body, as well as in the hands. You may even choose to place each object against the solar plexus or brow area in turn to help you determine which has been charged.

7. Between each session, replace all the objects under some running water or dip into a bowl of salt water to drain off the charge.

8. A new object is chosen, as is a different individual to try and psychometrize the group charge. Have fun with the exercise.

XIX: Creating the sacred chamber of touch

Meditation is a wonderful tool to enhance your own overall sensitivities. There are many forms and methods of meditation; one is neither better nor worse than any other. Some are more effective in serving specific purposes, however.

Most effective techniques of meditation—even for the development of psychometry—are simple. They depend upon capacities that can be developed and used by anyone, if some time and effort is applied. Everyone has the ability to achieve some results almost immediately.

Some meditations are passive, and some are active. With passive meditation, you learn to quiet the mind and body and allow images, and impressions to simply arise in the manner that the subconscious chooses. In a more active manner, we use creative imagination to send a message to the subconscious that we want only specific intuitive images and impressions—determined by our purpose.

All images, symbols, and ideas are linked to some archetypal energy in the universe. The subconscious mind monitors and mediates the play of all archetypal forces within our lives. On a meditative level, contact with the archetypal energy stimulates visions, impressions, feelings, and intuitive insights. If we meditate upon ideas and images of vibrant health, the archetypal forces are released more dynamically into our lives.

For this to happen on any level, we must use creative imagination. The images, symbols and ideas we create and use send a message to the subconscious to release all energies and impressions associated with the image.

It is the key to actively accessing and using your more intuitive energies. We create images and scenes within the mind associated with our purpose. These created images should take a three-dimensional form. They are often like a highly concentrated day dream—or even an actual dream.

With creative imagination in meditation, we train the perceptive faculties of the mind. When we fix the mind upon an idea or image with regularity, we grow more like that idea or image. This is an active, creative aspect of meditation. We become that upon which we reflect.

It is not important or necessary to meditate upon a wide variety of images, symbols and ideas initially to awaken and enhance your psychometry abilities. Rather, it is more important to concentrate on one symbol, image, or scenario and bring it into life within your subconscious and then the soul. This will, in turn, trigger a more conscious perception of all that we touch.

It only requires about 10 minutes a day of proper creative meditation to awaken greater perceptions. Once you begin this, do not break it off out of loss of interest or inconvenience. If practiced everyday for three months, you will achieve tremendous results. Then periodically repeat the process (at least once a week for another three months), just to reinforce it and keep it strong.

The following meditation is designed to increase your overall sensitivity to touch. It creates a space in the mind and consciousness where you can safely enter and open to higher sensitivities. It is a sacred chamber of the mind where you can access information about all that you touch and all that touches you. It is a place in which you are always protected and in control of what you experience on subtler levels. Because it is your sacred chamber, you can intensify or soften all that you feel to any degree you choose.

This sacred chamber is a place where supersensible impressions and intuition are translated into your conscious mind. It is a place of higher understanding of the conditions of life, people and all things that touch you and are touched by you.

This meditation opens the doors. After the images within it are imprinted upon the mind through its daily practice, you can enter it to consciously and more dynamically access your psychometry skills. Before handling the object to be psychometrized, simply close your eyes and visualize yourself within this sacred chamber. It will automatically open the doors of that level of the subconscious mind which is sensitive to impressions through touch.

This sacred chamber is yours. You create it and you can change it. In fact, you will find it changing, naturally adapting itself to you, as you become more developed in your psychometry abilities. Use the following meditation as a guideline only. Do not lock yourself into it. It can also serve as a powerful preparation exercise for doing any extensive psychometry work. I have found it especially effective to do before all psychometry demonstrations.

1. Begin the exercise by making sure you won't be disturbed. Take the phone off the hook.

2. Set the atmosphere. You may want to use an incense or essential oil in the fragrances that enhance sensitivity to touch, as discussed earlier in the book. You may also want to perform some hand reflexology or massage to sensitize the hands.

3. Close your eyes and relax. Perform a progressive relaxation or some form of rhythmic breathing. The more relaxed you are, the easier it is to access the subconscious mind.

4. Now visualize the following scenario. Imagine. Make it as real as you can.

Draw all of your energies in and around you, as if someone has placed an old comfortable quilt about your shoulders. You are relaxed and at peace.

Within the darkness of your mind a scene begins to form. You hear the faint sound of water—a soft trickling stream that must be near by. There is the sound of birds, and you can smell the gentle scent of spring flowers and new mown·hay.

You begin to feel the warmth of the sun upon you. It is soft and soothing. It warms the head and chest, and you can actually feel the individual rays touching and spreading throughout your body. It radiates from the chest outward in all directions. The warmth spreads down to your feet and up to the top of your head. It energizes and soothes you at the same time. You feel its energy touching and filling every cell in your body.

Your eyes are still closed, and you raise your face and hands to the sun. Your hands and face begin to gently tingle, as if coming to life. It is not uncomfortable, such as when your hand falls asleep, but they seem to awaken nonetheless. You begin to actually feel the air around you. No longer is it just empty space, but substance that is alive to your senses, and it is thrilling.

You open your eyes, and see before you a beautiful meadow. On the far side is a path leading down from a distant mountain to this meadow. The path is lined with flowers of every color. At the opposite side of the meadow, you see the path continue. It leads out from this meadow to a distant valley. As you look down this to the valley, you are able to see your present home within it.

You begin to realize that you are at a plateau, an intersection of time and space. It is an intersection where the finite and the infinite come together, a place of the physical and the spiritual. Knowing this is freeing to your senses. It relieves you of stress and worry. It is safe. In this place, you need only be and feel.

In the midst of the meadow is a large tent. The whole scene is like a picture of an oasis setting from the *Arabian Knights*. A soft breeze passes across you. As it touches your face, there are hints of images of where this breeze has passed before it touched you. It seems as if you can actually feel the memories within that breeze.

You notice that you are dressed in soft, loose fitting clothing. You are barefoot, and the grass is soft and lush beneath your feet. You can feel each blade of grass against your skin, and even the earth out of which it grows.

You step to the tent, and open its silken flap. It is soft and cool to the touch, and as you open it to peer inside, the inner fragrance of sweet scents fill your nose. It makes you feel a little giddy and childlike, and you can't help but smile. Its intoxicating scent draws you into the tent.

Your senses are alive. It is as if you are truly coming awake for the first time. Vision is clear. Sounds are soft and true. Fragrances are pure. Your entire body seems to have come to life.

In the background comes soft music from some unidentified source. Your body responds to each tone, as its carried through the air to you. It touches, caresses, tickles and soothes your body. Each note touches you like a gentle drop of rain from heaven.

The room is filled with thick lush cushions and pillows. You move into the center, and gently run your fingers across the silken fabrics. It is cool to the touch. And yet each pillow seems to have a life and energy of its own. Some seem to invite you to sit. Some to lie down, and others stimulate sexual feelings. Never have you felt so sensual. Every part of your body responds.

In the center of the room is a table upon which sit fruits and breads of various kinds. Upon it also sits a bowl of scented water to wash your hands in. You kneel beside the table and dip your hands into the water.

Your hands begin to tingle. Even though you cannot recognize the scents by smell, your hands seem to recognize that in this water is honeysuckle, sage and just a touch of sandalwood. You splash some upon your face, and then pat it dry with the folded cloth next to it. As you do, your mind is filled with images of those who made the cloth and the journey it took to become a part of this tent—a tent that was made especially for you.

In that moment you realize that you are in a

sacred chamber. It is a chamber in which you can feel anything you desire to whatever degree you desire. You are not sure how you know this, but you do—as surely as you know your name.

With each passing moment in this sacred place, your senses become stronger and more distinct. You close your eyes, and you see threads connecting everything and everyone in the universe. Nothing is separate. All things are connected. By heightening your senses—by learning to use this chamber—you can see connections in everything. You are reminded of an old axiom: "As above, so below. As below, so above." Nothing is separate, and it is in this sacred chamber that connections can truly be experienced.

You open your eyes with wonder at this inspiration. To test this, you pick up an orange from the table. You allow your fingers to run over its skin, and you even lay it against your cheek. As you do your mind is filled with images of orchards. You see the homes of the workers nearby, and you see the exquisite care of the trees and the picking. You see who picked this orange particularly and when it was done. And you know that with just a little effort, you could connect deeply into anything or anyone who touched it.

You lay it back down, and look about you. Never have you felt so connected to everything. Never have you truly realized that you feel everything. The softest thought carried through the air to the utmost emotion within a hug—everything is experienced by the body. It is simply a matter of opening oneself to it. If done in this sacred chamber, there comes with the experience understanding.

You know that this is a place where you can understand your feelings and experience them clearly. Here you can read and understand all that you touch and all that touches you. Somehow you know that with each visit your ability to touch more fully will grow. And this is comforting.

You cover your face with your hands, feeling new energy pulsing within both. Though you expected darkness with such a gesture, the light intensifies. You see yourself surrounded and permeated by light that ties you to all things within the universe. Everything around you seems to be swallowed up into that light.

You slowly remove your hands from your face, and the intensity of the light dims. As it does, you realize that the tent is gone. So is the meadow and all that you had experienced. And yet your hands and your face are alive, strong with feelings. And you realize that the sacred chamber you experienced lives on within your own light.

To bring it back, you need only relax, close your eyes, cover your face with your hands briefly. As you draw your hands away, it will draw forth out of you and form around you—a sacred chamber where you can touch all of life at its most intimate expressions.

❦❧

❦ 6 ❦

The Power of Empathy

One of the most heightened forms of clairsentience, and therefore psychometry, is empathy. Empathy is an infinitely more intensive response than that experienced through mere psychometry. It affects you more intimately and its effects can be more complicated. It enables you to experience others as they are beyond their outer faces, and it enables you to see yourself through the eyes of others.

How often have we all imagined what it would be like to be someone else and in their circumstances? We have all had these kinds of wonderings. Usually, we qualify them by imagining how we would respond, rather than seeing exactly how the other individual is truly feeling and experiencing these circumstances. And yet even when we do this, we are displaying the rudimentary ability to develop and express empathy. It is a reflection of the potential to heighten our sensitivity and to see the truth of all people and all things.

Empathy is often considered the most ancient of the healing arts. Legends and myths abound with individuals who took upon their own shoulders the aches, pains, and sins of others. Folklore around the world is rich with stories of those who could see through the eyes of others (including the eyes of animals). Most people have heard tales or stories of individuals who, by touching another's ache or pain, healed it. There are even tales of individuals who, by touching another person, are able to draw the illness into their own body and then transmute it there.

All of these—psychic healing, shapeshifting and more—are connected to empathy. It has many expressions. Only the major forms will be explored to any degree within this book. In spite of this, it is important to understand it—more so for anyone involved in the psychic field.

Everyone is naturally empathic. Life conditions and experiences can heighten, close, or even awaken it inappropriately. As with all psychic abilities, there are times and conditions that emphasize these skills. Unfortunately, if we are unaware of our ability, it can create problems for us.

Have you ever said, "I feel really strange today, and I just don't know why," or "I've been acting weird all week"? Such statements may reflect that you have empathically connected with others and not realized it. The emotions, attitudes, and feelings may not be your own. They may be what you have picked up from others you have been around.

Myths, legends, and tales reflecting empathy

Greek tale of Prometheus and the Stealing of Fire.

Christian tale of Jesus.

Eastern tales of Buddha's ascension.

Chinese tales of Kwan Yin.

Nigerian Tale of Nana Miriam.

German tale "Old Man and the Grandsons."

Irish tale "Half-a-Blanket."

African tales of Songi.

Greek tale of Orpheus and Eurydice.

Tales of the Mayan goddess Ix Chel.

Scandinavian "Tale of Tontlawald."

Celtic tales of Bridget.

American Indian tales of Changing Woman.

Grimm's tale of "Snow White and Rose Red."

East Indian tales of Kali.

Tale of "Beauty and the Beast."

Greek tales of Dionysus.

German tale "The Goose Girl."

Central African tale "Ki and the Leopard."

Celtic tales of Morgan Le Fay.

(These are but a small sampling of the myths and tales that reflect some of the aspects and expressions of empathy.)

With an empathic person, it is sometimes difficult to determine whether the feelings are one's own or someone else's. Even if the feelings have been picked up from some other person, an empathic individual will experience them as if they are his/her own. A truly empathic person is one whose body becomes the barometer for all that is experienced. Physical feelings, emotions and mental attitudes can so impress themselves and register upon you that you assume they are your own.

The best example I can give of this is in regards to a number of hypochondriacs I have counseled in the past. Most that I have encountered are very empathic. The aches, pains and illnesses they feel in their own body are what they have usually picked up from others they have been around. Their clairsentient ability is so strong that the illnesses register as if part of their own make-up.

Children are more naturally sensitive along empathic levels than adults. For most people, as we grow older, we build walls and cushions around us. We learn to become defensive. We have usually learned that such sensitivity in the modern world can make us vulnerable to others.

Several years ago, I stopped and watched some six to eight year olds playing organized baseball. At this age, the kids often don't hit very well, and several innings had gone by without anyone getting a hit. While I was watching them play, a small boy hit the ball to the outfield. His entire team jumped up, cheering and clapping. And more surprisingly, the team in the field was also so excited at someone hitting the ball, they jumped up and cheered too. As the ball rolled past one of the cheering outfielders, realization sunk in, and he ran after the ball. All of the kids felt the joy of that hit and responded to it. It was a wonderful demonstration of joyful empathy.

Most people have seen scenarios on television and in movies of children in a hospital nursery. The scene usually reveals one child becoming upset and crying. This in turn triggers a similar response in the rest of the children. This is an empathic response.

There was an incident when I was around 10 years old in which my father was chewing out and berating my older brother. I don't even remember what it was for, but I do remember as I sat in that room, I felt everything my father was expressing and everything my brother was feeling—anger, sorrow, frustration—all piled onto each other. My brother was crying and I began to cry also. My father turned toward me, eyes surprised and laughed, saying, "Why in the hell are you crying?" It was an empathic response.

There are many examples of empathic responses in society and our personal lives. Some are free, some are forced, and some are atavistic. When we cry at a movie, it is an empathic response. When we flinch at someone else being hit, we are feeling it on some level within ourselves. That is empathy. When we follow the trends, we are responding empathically. Advertisers use music and images to create empathic responses in those who listen and watch their commercials. If we are not aware of this manipulation, we are at the mercy of it. When we are able to feel a friend's ache and extend our arms to assist and comfort, we are expressing empathy.

Those with whom we are closest are the ones we will feel the most empathy for and with. We are connected to them. How often have we heard of husbands having sympathetic pains during their wife's pregnancy? This is empathy.

For those in the psychic and healing fields, it is important to recognize this natural human quality. It is so easy to connect to the problems and issues of those with whom you are working. Then you carry them with you, as if they are your own. It can be difficult to disconnect from the individuals you are working with.

Individuals who first begin to open to the psychic and intuitive perceptions find their innate and slumbering empathic abilities often awakened. Individuals who dream or experience visions of great catastrophes, such as plane crashes and such, are often experiencing an awakening of their empathic abilities. It is a natural part of our make-up and at times it will rear itself up to let us know it is still alive.

This often shows itself in other ways for the developing psychic. He or she may focus on one individual's problem. As a result of this recognition and focus, the individual may start encountering an increasing number of people with the same issue or problem. Uninvited intuitive flashes and even visions may occur in regards to that issue. I have heard psychics speak of times while watching the news of visions occurring that provide greater details to a particular story than what was presented on the television. This is an empathic response.

Even for those not in these fields, the stresses of co-workers are more easily picked up and taken home with us. Those who have difficulty separating work and home often need to do work on controlling empathic responses.

Some individuals that work closely with people have great difficulty separating once the work is completed. When I first began to work with locating lost or missing children and other people, I had great difficulty separating. I would feel what the individual went or was going through, and afterwards I would find myself in varying degrees of depression. I would not want to associate or deal with other people. I would wall myself off.

After a while, I found that I could not even look at pictures on milk cartons and such without knowing whether someone was alive, abused, or whatever. Even today, I still must practice some barrier techniques so as not to tie into such situations.

In the past four to five years I have learned to control my responses more effectively. It has taken practice and effort, but the efforts have been rewarded. I recently was asked to look into the death of a small child to see if there was reason to continue investigating. It took about 48 hours before I was feeling normal. The empathic response was still strong, but I am now able to recognize it for what it is and balance it much more quickly and easily. In the past, situations such as this would affect me ostensibly for at least a week to 10 days, and occasionally haunt me off and on for greater lengths of time.

Empathy has a wonderful synchronistic aspect to it. As we focus our energies along any line in life, we trigger ripples around us. This rippling sets up currents that take you along lines that bring you to important people and bring others along similar currents to you. These are usually individuals with whom we will have much in common. There is a natural resonance.

Empathy is a wonderful tool that can be used for diagnosis and insight into people, health and all of life. It is important though to develop it, strengthen it and control it. Empathic responses to life with no control or recognition of what is actually occurring will have you being tossed back and forth by whatever current in life you encounter. If we learn to recognize it and use it, we can read the currents and use them for our benefits. Working with the exercises in this chapter will help you with this tremendously.

How Empathy Occurs

Part of the reason for empathic responses is the auric field that we discussed earlier in the book. It has a strong dynamic electro-magnetic quality. We are constantly giving off and absorbing energy. Every time we come in contact with another person there is an exchange. We give them some, and they give us some. If we are not aware of this we can accumulate a lot of "energy debris." This can make us physically feel funny and even create emotional imbalances. We may even begin to feel like we are going a little crazy. Empathic people usually have a more dynamic magnetic quality to their energy.

The colors and clarity of colors in the human auric field will often reflect empathic individuals. Pink is one of the predominant determiners of strong empathic responses. This is especially true when it appears to be overlaying the face, hands and other parts of the body like a second skin.

Remember that our skin is our largest sensory organ. Pink is often a color used in color therapy to heal skin conditions. When it shows up in the aura overlaying the actual skin, it reflects a stimulation of the sense of touch.

Bright reds in the aura can also reflect a heightened sensitivity. Usually, especially if we are in the fire-red range, it will heighten all responses and can make an individual hypersensitive. Things said more loving are felt more loving; things said more cutting cut more deeply. With a lot of red in the aura, if someone looks at you cross-eyed, they might as well cut your heart out. You feel the full impact of whatever is being expressed around you, and you usually feel it physically.

Empathy is based upon *resonance*. Resonance is a term most often found associated with music. In music, it is the ability of a vibration to reach out and trigger a similar vibration in another body. This is most easily demonstrated through the use of a piano and a tuning fork. If we were to strike a tuning fork for middle C and feel softly along the piano wires, we would find that the piano wire for middle C would be vibrating in response to the tuning fork.

Every cell in our body is an energy resonator. It has the capacity to respond to any vibration or energy we encounter. In metaphysics we are taught that we are a microcosm of the universe. This means that we have all energies within us to some degree. Inherent within our physical and subtle energy fields are all the inherent energies of the universe. We have a capacity to resonate and respond to whatever we encounter.

An empathic response or resonance occurs when two or more bodies have similar or identical frequencies. If an individual is angry and his anger stirs you up, you are experiencing an empathic resonance. If someone's sexual arousal stimulates this in you, it is an empathic response.

Empathic responses usually occur in one of three ways:

Free empathic response: This occurs in individuals who are very compatible on many levels. Couples who have been together a long time enjoy free empathic responses. One partner feels and experiences what the other does. There is an innate resonance. An important factor in this is the readiness and willingness for the individual to respond. For those into metaphysics, in this lies the answer to the occult axiom: When the student is ready, the teacher appears.

Through empathic resonance, group rapport is established, and the individuals of the group are more able to respond to the energies of the individuals within that group. In groups that come together for a singular purpose, that purpose serves as the medium for establishing empathic resonance among the participants.

The second way is through forced empathic responses: Forced resonance occurs when two energy systems have different frequencies, and the stronger is transmitted to the other by force. This has both positive and negative aspects, and it does not necessarily have to be a physical force. A stronger force will move a weaker; an assertive force will move an unassertive.

Charismatic individuals are usually those who have a natural ability for stimulating empathic resonance in others. Their energy is so strong and so dynamic that they stimulate responses in others. Sometimes this is free and sometimes forced.

Individuals who attend lectures and readings are placing themselves, as I have mentioned, in a receptive position. They are opening themselves up to the possibility of being empathically influenced. There is no problem with this if the reader or teacher is legitimate, but unfortunately not all are. Being aware of this receptivity alone will help prevent this.

Individuals who respond to peer pressure—for good or bad—are experiencing forced resonance. The strength of the group overrides that of the individual. The combined force or energy of the group overwhelms the energy of the single individual and forces it into resonance with that group. It can be very subtle.

The third way is through atavistic empathic response: This is an uncontrolled empathic

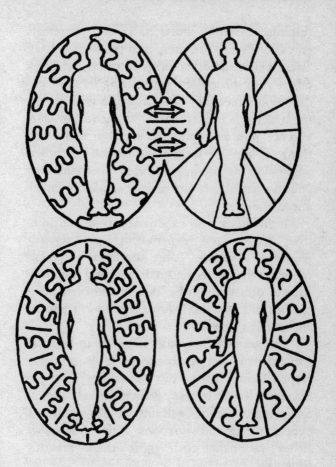

Energy exchange between auras

response. Some individuals are extremely empathic due to the circumstances of their lives. Stress, abuse and other forms of trauma can break down your auric field, puncturing it, short circuiting it. Since part of its function is to protect us, when it is broken down, weakened, or torn, you are more susceptible to everyone and everything in life. All feelings—physical and otherwise—will play upon you and be experienced by you more intensely and usually in a more unbalanced manner.

Individuals who experience uninvited intuitive flashes are experiencing an atavistic empathic response. Large numbers of people report having experienced dreams and visions of natural disasters, births, deaths and even plane crashes and such just before they occur. These are atavistic responses.

The atavistic response forces us to be more conscious of what we experience. It places greater responsibility upon our shoulders for our responses to life. In many ways it serves to protect us, giving us feelings and impressions about new people, places and situations. Unfortunately, we either rationalize or ignore these atavistic responses.

Empathic individuals need to pay attention to and honor what they feel. This is not always easy to do. We have not been trained to honor our intuitive aspects. Someone may appear to be O.K. He or she may sound sane, but with an empathic individual, it won't be until an actual physical touch occurs that a true assessment comes. The shaking of the hand or a brush up against will trigger the intuitive insights. It won't be until you actually touch the person that you will know where he or she is truly coming from.

Usually in those cases, the feelings are ignored or pushed aside. An individual may brush up against you, and all kinds of strange images and impressions may wash over you. The typical response is one of denial: "Why in the world would I ever think that of this person!" We don't honor what we feel, and it will often get us in trouble. Most of the time, those impressions are correct and will eventually prove themselves out, even if we don't understand them initially. The more we honor and acknowledge those feelings— that inner voice that is triggered through touch— the stronger it becomes each time thereafter.

EXERCISES

XX:Are you empathic?

The following questionnaire, although similar to that in the first chapter, will help you to determine more specifically if you have strong innate empathic qualities.

1. Are you easily persuaded or influenced by others around you?

(Empathic people are easily influenced and more susceptible to manipulation by others. They feel and experience what is projected towards them by others, so extra caution should be used when dealing with sales people and others who might manipulate. If you know that you are empathic, moving more slowly, not allowing yourself to be rushed and making sure you are completely comfortable will be more beneficial for you in the long run.)

2. Do your moods swing with whatever crowd or environment you find yourself in?

(Empathic people are easily drawn into the moods and energies of crowds. Often this is due to an expression of forced resonance. Remember that empathic people usually have a more magnetic energy field about them. They tend to absorb and take on the energy, attitudes and behaviors of the larger group, individuals and even environment. Awareness of this will help you to be less susceptible to this kind of influence.)

3. Do you ever find yourself "up" for a gathering or social event, only to find yourself shortly after arriving that you are feeling drained and tired?

(Empathic people must be a little more cautious in group settings. Because their energy is more magnetic, they can walk into a group and absorb the energy of whoever is present. Often, this kind of energy absorption occurs through the solar plexus. The individual picks up on all of the emotional and mental energy present, which immediately begins to weigh the individual down.)

4. Do you frequently find it difficult determining what you are feeling at any particular time?

(Because an empathic individual's mind and body is a living, breathing barometer for what the individual experiences, it can be difficult for the individual to determine whether the feelings are his/her own or what he/she may have picked up from someone else.

It is not unusual for most empathic individuals to actually feel and experience what others may project upon them. This may be another's attitudes, sexuality, and desires. This can be difficult, because usually such projections are experienced by the empathic individual as if they were his or her own feelings. Close, personal, and frequent monitoring is usually essential. The protection techniques in the next exercise will help with this.)

5. Do you frequently bring your work attitudes home with you or find yourself taking your problems into work? Is it difficult for you to separate work and home? Is it very difficult for you to be objective and separate issues and aspects of your life?

(If you find that you constantly bring work—attitudes and experiences—home with you to the degree that they affect how you deal with home life, then your empathic energies may need balancing. Even if it only occurs on rare occasions, it reflects a need to balance them. Remember there are cycles to our energies, and even our own innate empathic capacities have times when they are more active and more dormant, unless we learn to control them and direct them.

If you are one who has difficulty seeing people and life situations objectively, it can reflect a tendency toward strong empathic abilities. We all have periods in which this occurs; it is part of being human. On the other hand, if every aspect of our life is bleeding into every other, it indicates a need to control your energies more consciously.)

6. Do you consider yourself or do others consider you over-emotional? Do you cry easily (whether out of joy or sadness)?

(Empathic people are often over-emotional or hypersensitive. They respond more quickly and more strongly from an emotional base than other people. They laugh quickly and cry easily. They experience the full impact of whatever is being expressed around them.)

7. Are you hyper-sensitive, taking everything more seriously and personally than others?

(Things that might roll off the average individual's back are taken in and experienced fully by empathic people. Much of the reasoning for this was expressed earlier.)

8. Are you uncomfortable with other people touching you?

(Most empathic people can be placed in one of two categories, with most falling into the second. In the first are individuals who are the "touchy-feely" kind. They enjoy touching and being touched for the most part. Usually a part of them realizes also that through touch they are able to connect more truly with those they touch.

The second category is comprised of individuals who dislike being touched. They are so sensitive, that it is very uncomfortable to have individuals touch them, even with something as simple as a handshake.)

9. Are you, or were you, very shy and introverted while growing up?

(Most introverted and shy people are empathic. For many of them, this is a means of self-protection. On a subconscious level, they recognize that they can be affected easily by those they are around. They recognize that new people may have an energy that is unfamiliar and will be experienced strongly. Hesitancy to relate reflects this. And it is important to honor this. Others don't always know what is best for us, regardless of the intention. If we don't honor this, we never learn to develop and honor our own sense of self-esteem and intuition.

Unfortunately, we live in a society that is rather intolerant of such behavior. Parents and peers alike often push their children and friends into situations where they have to relate on some level. There is even a kind of stigma attached to being shy. In most cases, if the individuals are left alone, they will develop their own way of handling themselves more comfortably in social situations.)

10. Do you have a tendency to take on other people's problems, aches, pains, battles, worries, etc.—whether you are asked to or not?

(Often empathic people have to be careful about allowing themselves to be placed into situations where others unload problems and such on them constantly. We have all experienced this to some degree. How often have you felt drained or sucked dry after speaking with someone—even if only on the phone?

If this is occurring frequently, we need to examine why we are allowing ourselves to be placed in such a position. It often reflects that others are using—whether consciously or not — your empathic abilities to avoid their own issues.

At the end of such instances, the other person usually walks away with some of your more balanced energies, and leave you with theirs. You are then left with their problems and issues, trying to deal with them.)

XXI: Controlling and protecting empathic responses

Empathy is one of the most difficult abilities to control. It can be very confusing in that the individual is so easily influenced by others that discernment of one's true feelings becomes difficult. Exercise XX should have helped you to determine if you are truly empathic. Keep in mind, though, that there are various levels of empathy, but regardless of the level or kind, it can be controlled with effort and persistence.

It is important for anyone developing any psychic ability to cleanse the aura and energy on a regular basis. At some point you begin to truly realize that you are more than just a physical body. Most people focus their attention on only the visible and tangible, but science is proving everyday that we are affected by many things not visible to the human eye.

If you are unaware of how extraneous forces affect you, your own energy system can become weakened. This is even more true if you are in the least bit empathic. These weaknesses may manifest as actual physical illnesses or as mental/emotional imbalances. The key to preventing this from occurring is to strengthen and protect our auric field.

Most beneficial to this are general positive health practices. Proper diet, exercise, and fresh air are essential. On the other hand, lack of exercise, lack of fresh air, improper diet, abuse of alcohol, drugs tobacco, etc. create wear and tear on your energies and you are more likely to be affected by outside influences. The following will help you with this.

Let nature help you: Fresh air and sunlight is cleansing and strengthening to your energies. Spending regular time outside in the fresh air is balancing and healing. It will help you stay grounded and be less sensitive. Whenever you are feeling overemotional or sensitive in any way, get out into nature. Nature is always strengthening and insulating. It heals.

Go sit under a pine tree for five or 10 minutes. Pine trees are cleansing to the human aura. Their own energy fields serve to draw off negative emotions and balance out highly emotional states. In many ways, they use this negative energy debris almost like a fertilizer, so there is a nice balanced exchange that occurs.

Use cleansing exercises and techniques: Everyday when you shower and bathe, see it not just as a physical cleansing, but a washing off of the connections you have established in the course of the day. Remember: every time you interact with another, there is an exchange of energy. You give them some, and they give you some.

For empathic people, a bath or shower at the end of the day will be most essential to your overall health. It will help rid you of the debris you have accumulated throughout the day. It will help you discern what are your feelings and what aren't.

Use the following cleansing vortex exercise regularly. It will help you to keep a clear mind as to the energies you are experiencing. It will help you to define what are your feelings and what you may have picked up from others. In essence, it sweeps the aura clean, purifying you in mind, body and spirit.

- Take a seated position and perform a progressive relaxation.

- Close your eyes and in your mind's eye visualize a small, crystalline whirl-wind forming about 10 feet above your head. Visualize it as a tornado of pure white fire. As it forms a funnel shape, visualize it large enough to encompass your entire body and aura.

- Visualize this spiritual tornado moving steadily downward. The small end should be visualized entering into the crown of the head. It is then visualized descending through the body, encompassing it and the entire aura surrounding it.

- This whirlwind of spiritual fire should be visualized as rotating clockwise. As it touches the aura and the body, visualize it sucking off and burning off all of the energy debris you have accumulated from everyone throughout the day.

- See, feel and imagine it sweeping and cleansing your entire aura and body. As it moves through, allow this energy vortex to exit out through your feet into the heart of the earth itself. See this vortex carrying all of the debris into the lower realms, where it is used to fertilize and benefit the lower kingdoms of the Earth.

Learn to disconnect from others: It is most essential for empathic people to learn to disconnect from others. Ideally, this should be done immediately upon leaving a place or leaving the company of others.

I know I have repeated it often, but it is a critical point. Empathic people need to be able to separate their responses from others around them. Because they often experience others' aches, pains, feelings as their own, it can be difficult. Pay attention to what you feel when you touch or are touched by others throughout the day.

At the end of the day, look back over the day's events in reverse order. This reverse order forces you to concentrate on what you experienced and who you encountered throughout the day. You are less likely to skip over important details.

Everyone you encountered are individuals you need to disconnect from. With empathic people, the percentage is high that even in brief encounters you have connected to those you touched. The following will help you in this disconnection process and will enhance your own well-being:

- Wash your hands frequently throughout the day. For those who are in sales, healing, or positions where there may be a lot of hand-shaking and such, this is important. Empathics connect strongly through touch. Washing helps sever the connection, so that you do not stay connected the entire day with someone you shook hands with early in the morning.

- Visualize yourself disconnecting from others you encounter throughout the day. This can be done with each person as your encounter ends, or it can be done at the end of the day.

There are several ways of doing this. See all of those you touch being connected to you by thin lines of energy. Usually the connection is through the solar plexus, but visualize this line of connection in any way you find most comfortable.

Some people recommend seeing it as a cord that you pull out of your solar plexus area. Keep pulling it out until you can visualize the end strands. Then release it to be absorbed back into the other individual. You may even want to reverse it by pulling your energy out of the individual you touched, drawing your cords back so you don't lose your own energy in the process.

Some people simply see the lines of connections as threads that need to be cut. Visualize scissors and clip off the connection. This is a quick way, and can mentally be accomplished with each person you encounter throughout the day's activities.

Adapt it. Adjust it. Find the way that works best for you. If you don't find a way of disconnecting daily, you will find it difficult to determine whether your feelings are truly your own or what you have picked up from the others around you.

Even with loved ones this should be done regularly. With loved ones, the connections will easily reestablish themselves, so you are not going to do the relationship any damage at all. It will help you though to handle the relationship from a clearer perspective.

Use physical postures to protect yourself: There are natural energy currents throughout the body. There are ways of using physical posture to help keep empathics from becoming unbalanced, overly influenced, or even drained by others.

We have all experienced being drained by other persons. You may talk to an individual on the phone or in person, and, when you finish, you are exhausted. Or you find yourself taking on his or her problem. You may even find yourself being talked into things you didn't want to do.

These kinds of situations are easily corrected through simple postures and gestures which make you less susceptible to outside influences. These should be a part of everyone's regimen of psychic self-defense, whether they are empathic or not. In essence, they serve to close off the circuit of energy so that your energy only circles within your field and you are less likely to be impinged upon.

- The feet and hands are points where the major meridians of the body terminate, particularly at the toes and fingers. Cross your feet at the ankles. This will close off the meridians that go to the toes, and bring the fingers of the two hands together in a prayer position. Sit with your hands folded upon your lap. This closes down your energy.

Do this the next time you encounter your friend who always drains you or is always talking you into things. Then assume the position described. Keep it casual and simple, and he or she will not suspect anything. (It also works when you are on the phone.)

If you start doing this, it won't take but a few weeks before you get feedback. You may hear comments such as, "You are just not as nice as you used to be" or "You are not as open as you once were." This confirms that the posture worked.

You will still be speaking to them as nicely as ever, but you are not allowing yourself to be drained by them or overly influenced by them either. They may not understand the change, but they will notice—and so will you!

- Don't stand or sit directly facing individuals who have a tendency to influence you.

- When looking at and speaking to others, focus on their left eye rather than the right. The right eye is the sender for mental and emotional energies. If you focus on it, you are more susceptible to being influenced and empathically responding.

- When in group or one on one situations and you feel yourself being influenced—or even if going in you are aware there is greater likelihood of empathic responses—sit and stand with arms folded casually across the solar plexus. It serves as a guard against being overly influenced by the energies around you.
- Be aware of your aura as a shield.

XXII: Recognizing psychic currents

People provide clues as to attitudes and circumstances within their lives. Behavior, posture, movement, voice, appearance, fragrance—all serve to help you recognize an individual's psychic currents.

Psychic currents are the subtleties of life. They reflect the physical, emotional, mental, and spiritual states of the individual. Empathy, when developed and controlled, is a powerful tool for recognizing and reading these currents appropriately.

The key to reading these currents is learning to tune in to the other individual. Just as radio waves are picked up when the dial tunes to the appropriate wave-length, the human mind and body will as well.

For this exercise you will need another person to practice with. This is also beneficial to do in a group development situation, as the group members can switch around, and you get more practice.

1. Begin by doing a progressive relaxation. Remember this is not a test. Do *not* compare yourself to how others do; it will inhibit your natural responses.

2. Sit directly across from your partner. Initially, one will be passive, while the other does the attunement. At the end of the exercise you can switch roles.

3. The one who is to be read may find it more comfortable to sit with the eyes closed. (The next exercise will have you using eye contact to establish empathic connections.)

4. Focus your attention on your partner. Don't bore your eyes into him/her; simply keep a soft, focused gaze. You are going to connect with this person briefly to scan his/her well-being. To do this you will visualize a stream of light, like threads, linking your major energy centers (chakras) with his/hers.

Throughout this exercise, you will monitor not only your partner, but yourself as well. This is because your partner's feelings may register upon you as if they are your own. You may even wish to keep a notebook close by to record impressions.

Begin by visualizing a stream of light reaching out from the base of your spine to connect with your partner at this level. Once you see and feel yourself connected, ask yourself about the physical well-being of your partner. Are there any problems? As you do this, pay attention to anything you personally feel or experience. Are there tingles? Changes in temperature? Any emotions or feelings? Pay particular attention to any physical responses and where they occur in your body as you do this. Keep yourself relaxed. Focus on this for a minute or two.

Then move up to the area of your navel. Visualize a stream of light extending out from yours to your partners, linking you together at that level. What is he/she experiencing emotionally? What is your own personal, primary, emotional feeling at this moment? Joy? Anger? Distress? Wonder? Pay attention to anything you feel—as well as what you believe your partner to be feeling. Focus on this connection for a minute or two.

Move up to the solar plexus area. See yourself connecting with your partner on this level, just as you did with the others. Pay attention to any thoughts or ideas of inspiration. What are you thinking as this connection takes hold? What is running through your mind? Where are most of your partner's thoughts and mental activities focused at the moment?

Now move up to the heart. Link up with your partner in the same way as on the other levels. As you do, focus on what is the strongest desire in the heart of your partner at this moment. What dream is harbored deep within the heart? Trust what you feel.

As you connect next to the throat center of your partner, ask yourself what it is that he or she most needs to express. What is being expressed that shouldn't and what isn't being expressed that should? What is it you personally most wish to express?

Next, visualize and feel yourself connecting with your partner at the level of the brow. As you do, relax and allow yourself to be impressed. Are there any particular worries, fears or doubts arising? Any imaginative impressions, ideas and/or dreams?

Then as with the others, see a connecting of light form between the crown of your head and the crown of your partner. What do you feel needs to be asserted? Is the individual needing to assert himself/herself in new areas of life? Is the assertion too strong? What could be the crown of this individual's life activity?

5. After you have connected, just sit and focus in a contemplative manner on your partner. Don't try to get too specific. As you sit across from your partner, you will become aware of a mood, quality of thought or being. Don't aim for specific information. Initially, just try to determine general

impressions and feelings. Simply allow your partner's mood to pervade you until it actually becomes your own. You may feel your partner's anger, joy, apprehension, doubts, certainties, or any variety of feelings and moods. Do not try to interpret them. Just identify them and silently acknowledge them. You will be able to discuss them after the exercise with your partner. You will remember them.

6. Share the mood with your partner. Sometimes it helps to mentally wish to be of help to your partner in expressing or experiencing creatively the possibilities of that mood.

7. After about five minutes of this complete contemplation, draw back the connecting stream of light from your and your partner's crown. Absorb it back into your own body from where it originated. Do this in turn with each connecting link that you formed. As the last separation occurs, see yourself balanced, controlled and completely separated from your partner—with no residue other than memory.

8. Take time afterwards to discuss and share with your partner everything you felt or experienced. This feedback is essential to confirm and validate your impressions.

XXIII: Using empathy to create intimacy

The following exercise is very difficult to do. It requires a partner, particularly someone with whom there is a great deal of trust. It will help establish intimacy in relationships. Although it may seem easy, it is quite difficult. It requires allowing someone else to look into your soul, and you into his or hers.

This is an exercise that I sometimes refer to as The Way of Silence. It helps you to develop empathic and silent sight into others. It is a very intimate experience. With practice, it can be used with most anyone. Learning to shift into this silent soul sight is difficult to develop and control, but it has many benefits. The most obvious is that it enables you to truly see the world through the eyes of another.

In this exercise, you will sit, face to face, with another. I recommend that for the first few times that you do it with someone you truly trust. You will sit, totally silent and with eyes locked.

It is a most intimate experience in that you will sit and look into the eyes of your partner for several hours or even longer. As you do this, you begin to see the true soul of the other person and much of what it has gone through.

For most, using the Way of Silence can be very difficult. You will feel very exposed and may wish to avert the eyes or some such avoidance activity. If continued past this, there will come a point when you begin to see and feel what is being and has been seen and felt by the other.

For many people, this can be too much to bear, especially when the realization hits that the other is truly seeing and feeling what you have personally experienced in life. You actually begin to see the whole of a person's time in and through their eyes. This requires complete non-judgmental and unconditional acceptance and responses. If you do not think you can do this, do not even try.

For those just beginning, this exercise might best be performed in stages. Try it for 15 minutes initially; then gradually extend the time. For others in a relationship, you may wish to extend the time. It is essential to follow several rules:

1. There is to be no talking or commenting throughout the exercise. Verbal communication during the exercise will undermine your ability to truly feel and see through the other person's eyes.

2. Some physical contact should be maintained throughout the extent of the exercise. Sitting across from each other with knees touching is beneficial. So also is holding hands. It is important that both individuals be comfortable but touching.

3. Eye contact should be maintained throughout. It has been said that the eyes are the windows to the soul. This exercise will prove it. You do not have to stare intensely. It is not a staring contest.

Simply relax, gaze softly and gently into the other's eyes. Don't worry about blinking or the occasional shifting of the eyes.

If you find yourself or your partner averting the eyes, it is usually a clue that he or she is feeling vulnerable and that you are starting to enter into intimate areas of the person's life, whether you realize it or not.

Making your gaze more reassuring will help with this. Also you may even wish to smile softly or gently squeeze your partner's hand. To be able to truly see through his or her eyes, there must be safety and comfort.

Do not speak at these times, for that will separate the intimate feelings being established. It creates separateness. There will be time afterwards to speak, discuss, explain, and vocally reassure and comfort.

4. Each person experiences this silent sight in different ways. Some just feel things in their own body. Others see their partner's life playing before them like a movie. Some just experience the most important influences in shaping the life of the partner. Everything you feel and experience has validity.

As you experience these impressions about your partner, make a mental note and continue gazing into his or her eyes. Try not to reveal any response. Don't let your face reveal that you have experienced something. This will make your partner nervous. He or she will start to wonder what you saw or experienced, and it may make walls go up.

Don't try to force yourself into seeing through the other's eyes. You do not even have to imagine yourself looking out from behind them. Simply sit, gazing into the eyes, and it will all happen naturally. We are connected to all life, especially human, but over the years, we have built walls around ourselves to guard against our natural sensitivities. This exercise will confirm for you how naturally we can attune to others.

5. At the end of the prescribed time, stand and stretch. Each of you should take a turn and share everything that you experienced. While you share, the other person should remain relatively silent, other than to occasionally ask for clarification if needed.

After one shares, the partner should confirm and validate the feelings. Sometimes this may be done by providing details of scenarios or it may simply be by confirming events, feelings, and such. Then the roles are reversed.

Make sure that the exchange ends on a positive note. You will see the most intimate gifts, dreams and potentials of your partner whether they have been expressed in this life or not. You should encourage them. Both should remember that we are never given hopes, wishes or dreams without also being given opportunities to make them a reality. And the only thing that can shatter those possibilities is compromise.

XXIV: Alice in Wonderland

An exercise that is beneficial in developing your ability to resonate with a wider variety of individuals is one that I used to call Age Empathy but now I refer to it as The Alice In Wonderland Exercise. It helps you to develop rapport and resonance, while also awakening a greater flexibility in your own energies.

We live in a society that has a tendency to neglect and devalue two valuable groups—the very young and the very old. Child abuse is rampant, as is neglect of the elderly. In many ways the increase of this in modern times reflects an inherent tendency to numb our natural sensitivities or to allow ourselves to be socialized out of them. This is an exercise that will help prevent your natural sensitivities from atrophying.

With this exercise or any of the variations suggested, it is important to adapt them to yourself and your own life. Particularly with this exercise, it will enhance the overall effects.

In Lewis Carroll's *Alice in Wonderland*, Alice enters a room filled with locked doors. Behind a curtain she finds a tiny door that opens to a passage that leads out into a beautiful garden. On a table in the room is a potion marked, "Drink Me."

She drinks and shrinks small enough to walk through the tiny door out into the garden. Part of this adventure also involves her encounter with a tiny cake marked, "Eat Me." Eating it makes her grow large.

With this exercise, you visualize yourself at times both small and large. I don't recommend doing them within the same meditation time, but alternate them periodically. Grow small at one time, and large the next. You can also do it using age regressions and progressions. Instead of shrinking in size, see yourself becoming younger, going back to about five or six years old. When you eat the cake, see yourself aging by twenty, thirty or however many years.

It is important to try to see, feel, and experience everything from the size or age you become in the exercise. This will facilitate your being able to see and feel things in real life from other people's perspective. This enhances your natural empathic abilities.

1. Make sure you will be undisturbed. The phone should be off the hook and there should be no interruptions. Also as a preliminary to this exercise, it is beneficial to read the Lewis Carroll story, *Alice in Wonderland*.

2. Allow your eyes to close; breathe deeply. Perform a progressive relaxation, sending warm, soothing thoughts and energy to every part of the body.

3. Visualize yourself as Alice. See yourself as her size and age. You think as she thinks. You speak as she speaks. Your curiosity and imagination are as vivid as hers.

4. As you focus on this, a large white rabbit runs by you. And you follow it down its hole. It is dark at first as you descend, but then it grows brighter. Before long it empties into an immense chamber.

The room has a table in the center. Upon the table are a variety of apothecary bottles and miniature cakes. At the outer edge of this chamber are doors of different sizes, shapes and contours. One is very tiny, and you know you would have to be no more than 10 inches tall to go through it. One is so large that even as an adult, you would not be able to reach its doorknob. Another seems ancient, while yet another seems new. Each door has its own character that reflects the kind of experience you would encounter by walking through it.

You move to the table, and in the center is the only apothecary bottle that is marked at this time. In front of it is a small card upon which is written in an ornate scroll, "Drink Me." Somehow you know it is safe, even though you know it will also open a new experience for you.

You uncork the bottle, and take a tiny sip from it. It teases the tongue with its exotic sweetness, and it warms and relaxes the throat as you swallow. There is a soft, pleasant tingling sensation, and a tiny giggle escapes from you. You smile, close your eyes and drink down the remaining elixir.

When you open your eyes, you find that everything around you has become huge. You are dwarfed by the table. As you stand at the bottom of its one leg, it seems as if you are standing next to a giant oak tree. There is no way you can reach the top of the table. It is then that you realize that you have shrunk.

You move toward the only tiny door in this chamber. As you open it you step through and onto a path. The path leads you into childhood scenes, like an experiential museum. You watch yourself in different childhood scenarios as you walk along this path, remembering and reconnecting with those parts of you.

You remember what it was like to be smaller than everyone else. You see adults walking around you, appearing as giants. You remember how strange and different you felt from everyone else. You see your bedroom and your old school, and you remember what it was like to walk into a new place, and how large it all seemed at the time.

Allow yourself to feel and experience it, to remember what it was like to be small, to be a child. You will see with a child's eyes and experience it all from a child's physical perspective, but you will still have your adult mind to keep you safe, relaxed and balanced.

You may wish to relive in this one or two childhood experiences. As you begin to realize and remember what it was like to be this small, you come to the end of the path. At the end is a large door, with a handle too tall for you to reach. At the foot of the door is a small table just your size. In the center of the table is a tiny cake with a card in front of it which reads, "Eat Me."

You take a bite, and you feel a wind building around you. You close your eyes and finish the small cake. Your body tingles pleasantly, and you can feel yourself stretching and growing. You open your eyes, and you see you have returned to your normal size.

You laugh to yourself and look back along the path you had just walked. Now everything seems so small. Your room and school really wasn't so big. It was all in your perception at the time. The adults seem smaller and less alien to you.

5. You breathe deeply, relaxing, then you open the door and step through. You allow your eyes to stay closed as the scenario begins to slowly dissipate and fade. You are feeling relaxed and balanced, but you are very aware of how it feels to be small and young once more. You know that you will never forget, and that you will be able to make those who are in such a position more comfortable with it.

❧

❦ 7 ❦

Techniques for Psychometry Readings

Developing psychometry does not qualify you to do psychic readings or consultations profession-ally. There are many applications for the personal use of your ability within your day-to-day life. I have been seriously involved in the metaphysical and psychic field for over 25 years. In that time I have come across wonderful psychic counselors. I have also encountered some who were absolutely garbage.

How do you tell the difference? It is not always easy. Anyone can open up and provide psychic/intuitive information. This alone in no way qualifies someone to be a counselor or advi-sor to others. Equally, if not more important, is how that message is communicated. Is it empow-ering and helpful? Is it delusionary? Does it imply a lack of free will? Does it help resolve issues in productive ways?

These are just a few of the many questions you should ask yourself when involved in a psychic counseling session—whether as client or as the reader. Later in this chapter will be more involved guidelines to test yourself or those you visit.

In the past seven to eight years, there has been a tremendous influx of people into this field. More than a few have merely read a few books and/or taken some development seminars and assumed it qualified them to use their psychic abilities professionally and publicly. Unfortunately, it is often to the detriment of other, more qualified, professionals in the field.

Today, we have more knowledge of the workings of Nature and the human mind than at any time in history. We are breaking into the mysteries of the universe that have previously been hidden. We are more understanding of the psycho-structure of the human mind in ways never before comprehended. Knowledge of every aspect of humanity is more plentiful today.

In ancient times, mystical and metaphysical knowledge was hidden from the general public. The awakening and use of higher levels of consciousness was overseen by a teacher or master. Today, this knowledge is more available. Because of this greater knowledge, there is also greater responsibility. Because of the prominence of information and knowledge available, humanity does not need a teacher to open the doors to other dimensions and levels of consciousness.

There is, however, the same responsibility. The spiritual student must win for himself/herself the conditions necessary for developed higher consciousness. This requires great time, energy and effort. It requires a genuine search and use of knowledge. It requires greater depth of study of all the spiritual sciences. There should be complete and independent testing by the individual. This includes the ability to draw correspondences and see relationships. It also includes the ability to discern and discriminate the truth from the half-truths and the illusions from reality. It involves being able to take the psychic information and apply it productively and creatively for yourself or for others. The more educated you are, the more effective you will be with your counseling if you choose to do so.

This process is time-consuming, and we do live in a "fast-food" society. Few are willing to put forth the amount of time, energy and training that is truly required to be an effective psychic counselor.

Unfortunately, many "psychics" believe that stepping out onto a professional path will move them further along the spiritual path of life. This is a misconception prevalent throughout the metaphysical community. There is an underlying assumption that if you are not working actively in the metaphysical field, then you cannot be making spiritual progress.

The two do not go hand-in-hand. In fact, stepping out publicly too soon is more likely to set you back, eventually bringing upon you some tough lessons. Many believe that if they are not demonstrating publicly their psychic abilities that they are not growing. As a result, there now exists a preponderance of individuals trying to teach and work in the field with neither the proper depth of knowledge nor the experience. It creates problems for both themselves and those who come to them for assistance.

The most obvious problems occur within the physical and the financial. Health of the body, mind and/or spirit will decrease. Financial difficulties surface and increase. Life becomes increasingly complicated and difficult to handle. Stress increases, while the individual's ability to handle stress effectively decreases. If ill prepared, these problems will usually manifest in three to seven years. I have seen many individuals "spiritually explain" these conditions away as being part of their own higher initiation, rather than seeing it as it really is, a lack of preparedness.

Unfortunately, there are always those simply looking to hang out their own shingle. For some of them, it is a way of saying to themselves and to their friends, "Look at me. I'm special." For others, it is a way of adding some glamour to what they perceive as dull and unproductive lives. Some even use it to assert their own spirituality to the world.

Often, those with just a little bit of knowledge, the psychic dabblers, feel they are constantly in control when in reality they are not. Frequently, the true realizations do not occur until it is too late. Uncontrolled fancy is a term that applies to many who have stepped out into the metaphysical field in more recent times without proper preparation. This is the ability to discriminate illusion from reality.

Everyone should pursue their dreams, but to pursue it without preparation will bring catastrophe. Psychic impressions, visions, channelings and insights can be nothing more than uncontrolled fancy, a manifestation of your imaginings to provide a stroking for the ego.

Not delving deeply enough, accepting blindly without testing, failing to be objective in the process of self-observation can lead to uncontrolled fancy. What may come through as a spiritual insight may be little more than a fanciful manufacturing to verify what you already know or to justify your own actions or thoughts.

Creative imagination is important in unfolding our higher potential, but it must be controlled. Sometimes the difference between it and uncontrolled fancy is difficult to detect. This is why continual self-observation and in-depth preparedness is essential. It is to easy to screw up another person's life, let alone your own.

There is no fast and easy method along the spiritual path. Even the path of our dreams requires persistent effort, much time and energy.

Our dreams cannot be fulfilled by mere clairvoyance or demonstrations of psychic power. "Remember that what is psychic is not always spiritual. What is occult or metaphysical is not always uplifting, and what is appealing is not always useful to us."*

Over the years I have seen a large number of individuals who have fallen prey to this particular expression of uncontrolled fancy. They have a vision of working in the field and find that their efforts are blocked, hindered and filled with financial and spiritual setbacks. Most often, these failings occur because the individual(s) involved was ill-prepared to begin with, tried to do too much too soon (expecting it all to fall into place with little effort), or simply did not persist.

Many of these individuals have since given up entirely, bewildered at how they could have been misled by their visions. Their visions and dreams may have been true, but for dreams to manifest there must be proper development, preparation and persistence on all levels. The foundation upon which they were building their dream had not been laid.

I am frequently asked how things fall into place so easily for me. The truth is, they don't. It only appears that way to the outside observer. I have studied and worked seriously for over 25 years. Prior to the age of 15 I was a dabbler and a

* Andrews, Ted. *Imagick.* Llewellyn Publications, St. Paul, 1989

game player with the psychic realm, but I began to explore in a concentrated manner. It required more time and effort, as there was not a great deal of information available when I first began. Much of it for many years was trial and error.

I also have an educational background that includes ancient literature and linguistics. This placed me in a position to study and explore teachings of other times and places. I worked full time as a teacher and counselor for ten years. I made sure I was schooled. The greater and more in-depth schooling, on any level, the greater the potential for being a physically, emotionally, mentally, psychically and spiritually creative person. The learning never stops. The training and developing is continual.

A truly creative psychic counselor is one who can process and apply the information in new ways. You will intuitively see possibilities for transforming ordinary data and experiences into new creations. You will help yourself and others to see the creative possibilities within life situations, no matter how trying they may be.

It is important to remember at all times that to demonstrate the psychic without proper awareness of how to apply that knowledge beneficially, makes that ability impotent. If only for this reason, training in counseling is always advisable for anyone working publicly. This training can be achieved in a variety of ways:

- Take some night courses in psychology and counseling at a local college.

- If you cannot afford to attend the classes as an actual student, audit them. You will still get training; you just won't have any accreditation for it.

- Take some classes in public speaking, interviewing, etc. Learn how to speak to people.

- Volunteer for local help-lines, providing assistance and information over the phone. It provides wonderful experience in developing flexibility in communicating to a wider variety of individuals. You will need to adjust your style of speaking.

- If you are seriously thinking about becoming professional, regularly work at psychic fairs and the like, doing mini-readings. These force you to shift from one person to the other quickly so that you develop your ability to turn your psychic intuition on and off at will. It also brings you into contact with a wider variety of people, so that you learn to adjust your approach. It also strengthens your ability to connect and disconnect from others, and builds up your own energy so that doing readings is less draining. Psychic fairs can be a wonderful training ground. You can never make a living at them, but they open doors and provide development opportunities.

Over the years, I have seen many psychic aspirants attempt "to be" before they have learned "to become," and it does trip them up eventually, resulting in imbalance for themselves and often for others. Psychic knowledge is worthless unless it is integrated into your life in a balanced and creative manner. This is why the process of "becoming" is so critical to the spiritual/psychic student. Through it we learn to integrate all levels of our life.

This was part of the task of the ancient mystery schools. It is why silence was often required in the early years of their concentrated study. They taught that it was the fulfillment of our daily obligations in a creative manner that propels us along the path. It is not the demonstration of psychic ability or book learning that unfolds our potential. In fact, it can hinder us in the early years of development. Rather than concentrating and focusing that new energy, many dissipate it by using it to "teach" or "be psychic" prematurely. The need or desire to be out front can get in the way of our higher good.

It is through the daily trials and tests that we begin to unfold our sleeping potential. For many, this will simply involve opening the hearts of those they touch on a daily basis with a smile, a kind word or the meeting of obligations. You may not demonstrate your knowledge outwardly or receive the attention that others do, but this does not imply that you are any less evolved. It may indicate that you do not need to learn how to be out front. You may have other lessons more essential for your soul's growth.

For many, the life quest will take shape by working and teaching within the metaphysical and spiritual fields as we know them today. For others, it will simply take the form of living their daily lives in a creative and productive manner. It will involve using those inner potentials, such as psychometry, to be a positive influence in the lives of those they touch.

One purpose of psychic development is to open new perceptions, to look beyond physical limitations. It helps you learn creative possibilities that exist within limitations, while at the same time transcending them. It helps restore the wonder, awe and power of the Divine and life. Instead of looking for some light to shine down upon you, you realize the light that can shine out from you.

Hints for Receiving a Psychic Reading

Most people who do psychic counseling have been through the process themselves. They have usually had good readings and bad. For anyone going to an intuitive, a psychic counselor or a medium, there are important things to keep in mind. These should be reviewed and considered before going to such a person, and they should be used afterward also to help you more objectively evaluate the experience.

1. Choose the psychic carefully. Ask for recommendations from friends and associates, but also keep in mind that the level of rapport with a psychic will vary. In the beginning, or if you are in need of further confirmation, visit more than one. See how they compare.

2. Psychic fairs can be a wonderful way to find individuals who will be good to work with psychically. They are inexpensive and you can get an actual sampling of a variety of readers and methods. Psychic fairs are often used to introduce people to readings. They are meant to be fun and entertaining. They are often a training ground for developing psychics. They are not places to resolve major issues in your life. They can also be great places to pick up on word-of-mouth references.

3. Initially, avoid the psychic telephone lines. It is best to have in-person consultations. That way

you can assess more effectively the credentials and abilities of the individual. Since with most phone line services you pay by the minute, it is not a good time to get references which are necessary.

4. Know what method(s) the psychic uses before hand. You may even wish to get several kinds to decide which you prefer.

5. Always ask for references. Don't be afraid to ask how long an individual has been practicing. If the psychic seems offended or makes you feel foolish in any way for asking, it is a strong indication that something is probably not right. Ask what their specialties are, what you can expect and how accurate it will be. Ask about their educational background as well. The more information you have, the easier it will be to assess the legitimacy of the individual.

6. Always inquire of the fees beforehand. A higher fee does not make the individual a better psychic. Make sure that at the end you feel comfortable with what you paid for. Be wary of individuals who charge exorbitant fees. There is nothing wrong with charging an equitable price, but it is in no way an indication of the person's ability.

Readers who socialize too much during the reading time are taking advantage of you. If you pay for a half hour, get a half hour's worth of effort.

7. Be cautious of psychics who stroke your ego with fantastic past lives, exotic promises and pre-

dictions. *Get up immediately and leave if the reader predicts a death or such.* The only one who knows truly when a soul will leave its physical life is that soul itself. Up until that moment there is free will. A psychic who tells of this can easily plant a seed whose energy may help manifest it.

Yes, as a person becomes closer to that transition called death, there are certain signals that will indicate it. A good psychic counselor will present the information in a manner that will not frighten and will help the individual to prepare for all possibilities. If the reader cannot do this, he or she has no business serving as a counselor.

8. Be cautious of psychics who claim they can remove your problems and solve your issues, alleviate your shadows or get rid of "bad spirits" with psychic and occult techniques. The only thing that will be removed will be the money from your wallet or purse.

9. Do not visit a psychic too frequently. Be very wary of psychics who go out of their way to make you come back. I personally rarely see anyone more often than every 10-12 months. Usually, there is not enough change to warrant a full reading before that. I tell my clients that if something important comes up, I will take care of it over the phone (with no charge).

Seeing a reader too frequently is a way of avoiding responsibility. You are allowing the reader to direct your life rather than living it yourself. There should be no reason to consult a reader every week or month or for everything that surfaces.

10. Be skeptical of those who only depart negative information, or who are constantly asking you questions rather than relaying information. Some readers also spend a good part of their client's time telling the client about the psychic successes with other clients. Some have a tendency to give little information. Remember you are paying for their services, make sure you get your money's worth.

I rarely ask any questions in my readings. I am not looking for confirmation or to prove myself to the client throughout the reading. Unfortunately, some readers do this to make sure their clients are truly impressed.

11. Be aware of the health and vitality of the reader. If the reader has health problems, it will color the information that comes through. Some readers look like they have been staring into a crystal ball much too long.

12. It is most important to remember that you will be placing yourself in a receptive position. You are more open to being influenced in such situations. You don't want to be skeptical and test the reader throughout, but do not accept everything as it is presented. Remember that ultimately no one knows better for you than you, no matter what their credentials or reputation may be.

13. Do not be afraid to ask questions. The more specific your question, the more specific answer you should expect. If something does not make sense, file it away. You do not have to continually express skepticism or be antagonistic, but a cautious optimism is beneficial.

14. Examine your needs and motives for visiting a psychic. Are you looking for a quick fix or for someone to tell you what to do with your life? Are you looking to for a way of avoiding responsibility? Are you hoping to discredit the psychic? Are you looking for lucky numbers and such to obtain instant wealth? Are you seeking a psychic's solution when maybe you need a therapist's help and guidance? Are you looking for insight so that you can take the most appropriate action(s) for yourself?

15. Don't force the psychic's impressions to fit your life circumstances. Most of the time, they will either fit or not fit. If you offer to the psychic a possible explanation for his/her impression and find them constantly shifting to make it fit with what you have said, warning bells should sound.

Granted, there will be information that surfaces that seems to have no connection to anything in your life. Don't necessarily accept it blindly or negate it immediately. File it away for now. In time, it will either prove itself or not. Reputable psychics will do the interpretation for you and not expect you to do it.

Nothing aggravates me more than when I hear a psychic tell someone something like: "I see this beautiful silver cloud forming around you. Do you know what this is in reference to?" Then, when you provide a possible point of reference, they hone in on it. A reputable psychic will rarely need your input to interpret the symbols and impressions he or she is receiving.

Applying common sense to getting a reading or psychic counseling is essential. Seek a psychic's help at a time when you are relaxed and undisturbed. If not, try to put your mind at ease. The more relaxed you are, the easier it will be for the psychic to attune to you.

Permit the psychic counselor to proceed in his or her manner. Do not expect your first problem to be discussed and resolved at once. Every psychic has his or her own way of proceeding. Avoid comparing psychics during a reading. Don't tell your reader what another reader told you.

Don't try to confuse your reader. Rarely will a reputable psychic want or need help. Letting him or her know when they are correct is always helpful. Skepticism and arguing will lead to failure.

Do not be too quick to deny something presented to you. You may not understand it at this moment, and maybe the psychic will be able to clarify more specifically for you.

A reputable psychic will make possible predictions, but you always have free will. Your own actions or lack of actions will manifest certain conditions. A good psychic will help you to see those possible options or courses. Guidance is the key. A psychic reading is not fortune telling.

When you have been to a legitimate and reputable psychic, the information presented will go beyond that which is arrived at in natural boundaries of life. The reader will present information or events with which you can associate. Does the information apply to you? Is it inconsistent with other things mentioned by the reader or just different? Does the reader speak only in generalities or are you given specifics? I usually start generally, and move into very specific information, but even the general information will fit closely 90-95 percent of the time, while the specific will usually run a little higher. Remember that different psychics operate in different manners.

Occasionally, there will be contradictions. I know of no psychic who ever claims to have the whole picture. The long term record of a given psychic is a more significant factor than a short term contradiction with another psychic. Remember that a reputable psychic counselor will help you see the major issues of your life more clearly and help you to understand the repercussions and implications of various courses of action open to you.

Most psychics have days in which they may not be as "on" as usual. This must be considered. It is often a subjective point. As part of my readings, I give a yearly forecast, a month-by-month outlook of possibilities of what the client can look forward to. In this forecast I usually mention specific dates and their significance to the individual. There have been times in which I thought I wasn't on at all with the dates, but I never change anything I have given nor do I look for ways of explaining them if they do not turn out. It is not unusual to feel I have been off, and then later I would be informed by the client that I had been nearly 100 percent accurate.

Psychics are human too. Daily stress, emotions, diet, illness, alcohol and drugs all will affect the ability of a psychic to perform up to peak standards. Everyone is susceptible to off days. Psychics are no exception.

You should always come out of a good psychic session energized. You should feel positive and more in control. Regardless of the issues in your life, you should feel better prepared to handle them. A good psychic counseling session is always healing.

Basic Counseling Guidelines

This section will not make you a legitimate counselor, but it may help you become a little more effective with your psychic consultations. This is a composite of a variety of communication tools that will make you more effective in handling people beneficially in counseling situations. Again, I heartily recommend that if you are doing professional psychic consultations, even if you have been doing it for years, to seek out some formal education and training in interpersonal communication and counseling. We can all work toward improving our techniques of presenting assistance to those who come to us for insight.

When I first began teaching school, I was fortunate enough to fall into an innovative program to deal with high school students who had either been kicked out or dropped out of the regular high schools. In many ways they were disadvantaged—socially and economically. Our task was to employ remedial education so that they could reenter the traditional schools or provide vocational training so that at the very least they would become employable. Needless to say, there were many discipline problems.

The vocational teachers had little background in educational techniques. They were individuals who had spent their lives in the work force, but they had little formal training in teaching or with classroom discipline. To assist them I put together a small manual and workshops for our center on how to instill and restore discipline in the classroom. The techniques were based on simple and effective communication and counseling skills that anyone could apply successfully with a little effort and patience.

The techniques that they learned are techniques that anyone should learn and apply if they intend to present themselves to the public as an adviser or counselor in any fashion. Some of which follows includes the skeletal framework of those same techniques that I presented to the instructors at the center. They are as effective now as they were then, and they have application in any field of interpersonal communication.

The following guidelines are most effective when used in conjunction with each other. We don't have to be perfect in all of these; none of us will be. We can, though, work towards some goal of perfected application. At the very least it is good to periodically review them and ask ourselves how effective we are in applying them.

Make your expectations clear: Let your clients know what they can and cannot expect from your consultation. Offer your credentials, and be prepared to present references. Hesitancy to share your own background will make them hesitant to trust you.

Let them know costs and the time involved. Be consistent with fees. If you charge one person one price and a different price for someone else, it will get around. If you are charging a regular fee, make sure you are worth it. And make the fees reasonable. Exorbitant fees are an outrage, and it in no way indicates the quality of the consultation you will receive.

Let the clients know ahead of time if they can record. Let them know everything they will need in order to experience an enjoyable and beneficial psychic counseling. Make sure they know what kind of consultation you will be doing with them.

One aspect of making your expectations clear is not to have surprises for your clients. Many readers still use a tremendous number of props: the darkened room, a crystal ball for show, incense that chokes, exotic and ridiculous costumes and such. Indulging in theatrical atmospheres will often disturb your clients and will do nothing to enhance your reputation. Mostly it only serves to make clients uncomfortable.

Let the atmosphere of your place of counseling reflect a comfortableness. This sets a tone of professionalism and concern which will put your client more at ease. This in turn facilitates your own intuition.

Be consistent: Treat everyone with equal respect and consideration. No two people are ever going to be alike, but you should employ the same format and behavior with all to the best of your ability.

This especially applies to the time and energy you use in your consultations. If the reading is to be a half hour make sure it is that. Always try to stay as close to the time designated as possible. If you have other clients waiting, it is unfair for them to wait because you overrun with another client.

Yes, sometimes it does happen, but schedule well enough that you can eliminate as much of this as possible. I always leave a 15 minute interval between the end of one session and the beginning of the next. This allows extra time for unusual circumstances that can arise during a consultation or the occasional late arrival.

Also make sure your clients know that you hold to the timeframe as closely as possible. If they are late, it is not fair to put the next client behind schedule. If they know this and know you will hold to this, they will rarely ever be late.

Occasionally, you will have people in distress that will require more time and energy. Don't rush them through simply because you another client coming. Be prepared to be set back periodically, as you will encounter sad and desperate people who will require more time and energy.

Respect the individuality of the client: Talk with them, not to or at them. Don't embarrass or preach to them. Direct them. Provide guidance and suggestion. Allow them to ask questions. Remember that they must live their own lives. You cannot do it for them. Ultimately the consequences of their actions and behaviors—good, bad or indifferent—fall onto their shoulders alone. Help them understand this.

If you work as a professional psychic consultant, you are placing yourself in a position of great responsibility. You also forfeit some of your own rights. You, obviously, cannot be late for appointments. You should never be rude, impatient or disapproving, no matter who the client is. You will be encountering a wide variety of individuals. Some you will like; some you will not.

Learn to develop detachment. Remove your own opinions and personal judgments. It is not easy to forget yourself when consulting with some individuals, but if you are truly interested in being professional and developing a high degree of accuracy, you must develop a detached ability to deal with the public on a day to day basis.

All situations have choices and options: There are always choices and options available. What you receive intuitively is not written in stone. It is not predestined. Most clients will simply need to see and understand possibilities so that they can make appropriate choices. Part of your task is to intuit those possibilities and present them.

Everything in life involves choice. Through the client's choice, he or she creates or helps manifest certain situations—good or bad. Help the client see the choices, the alternatives and the consequences of their decisions.

A client should always leave your session more positive, empowered, and energized than when he or she came in. He or she should be in a better position to handle life and all its situations. Remember, it is your task to provide a forecast that is as sensible and as accurate as possible. It is not your task to give personal opinions.

If a client presses you, remind them that you are not a professional therapist and thus your opinion is only your opinion, with no more weight than anyone else's. Keep in mind that as a reader, anything you say to anyone about anything is going to take on much greater importance to the client—whether it is of substance or not.

Use encouragement or suggestion: It is not your role to lead the life or make the decision for your client. Presenting information in encouraging and suggestive ways is more empowering to the life of the client. Ultimately the responsibility for the individual's life falls into his or her hands. All you can do is guide and suggest.

Don't intrude upon the free will of the individual. The choices and actions are the client's alone. Resist telling them what to do. Suggest, hint, guide and show possible repercussions of different courses of action, but allow the final choice to be the individual's. It empowers them and demonstrates a respect for their own ability to handle life effectively.

There is always more than one way of performing tasks and resolving situations. Some might be easier than others. Let the clients know their choices. Offer suggestions for resolution and the reasoning behind suggestions, but leave the choice up to them. Allow your clients the opportunity to make their choices, even if it means making some mistakes. Sometimes people only learn and grow the difficult way. Experience can be a good teacher.

Cultivate a good sense of humor: Many clients will come to you with tragic situations. It can be easy to take responsibility and ownership of their problems. A good sense of humor will help prevent this.

Don't be afraid to laugh with the client. Private consultations can be serious, but seeing the humor or irony of situations can be very healing. A good laugh (not at the expense of the client) is good for the body and mind.

Do not allow your humor to become a mockery of something sacred to the client or to his/her shortcomings or failings. If you joke with the client, make sure the client knows you are joking. Don't allow the joke to come out as a criticism of his/her behavior.

Use a sandwich technique: Start with the positive aspects of your client and their life situations. By beginning with this, it will be easier for the clients to accept information that may not be as positive. This also reinforces the self-esteem and puts the client more at ease with you.

Then discuss troublesome areas or those that may need improvement. Keep it a discussion.

Present what you see or feel, but do not preach or hammer on those areas or what you would do if you were in that position. You aren't. Present options, choices and possible ensuing events from the choices that could be made. Allow the client to provide his or her own input.

Always conclude on a positive note. No matter how difficult the life situation, the individual must know that there are positive opportunities and options. As the psychic counselor, it is your task to help them with this.

By using this technique you magnify the positive and minimize the negative. If the client feels that you can see some positive benefits in him/her or the situation and its outcome, he/she will begin to build upon and act on that belief.

This does not mean that the negative should be avoided or not given, but by beginning with appreciation for the unique characteristics and qualities of the individual, and then by making suggestions that the clients can understand and work with, you contribute to their growth and not their further disillusionment.

Be tactful: Tact, diplomacy and grace are sometimes difficult to develop. Much of it comes through experience. The more you meet and work with people, the easier it will be to find your style that is most effective for difficult situations or issues in a person's life.

Be tactful in presenting negative information that you are impressed with. Remember that there is always the possibility you may be wrong or may interpret your impressions incorrectly. It is very easy to influence someone in ways that can be detrimental without realizing it. Be gentle.

No reading is perfect: Some may come close, but there is always room for improvement. Unfortunately, you won't always get feedback. Sometimes the only way you know how accurate you are is if the person comes back for another consultation later or if friends of the client call for appointments as well.

Question yourself constantly. How could your readings be improved? What could you do to make the consultations more perfect or beneficial to the client? What can you do to help the clients feel more empowered?

It is generally not a good idea to rehash readings. Such activities have a tendency to keep you tied into the individual or to take their problems upon yourself. On the other hand it is beneficial to periodically review a consultation or two. Could you have phrased something better? Could you have said or done something in the reading more effectively?

The quality of your sessions are going to vary. Sometimes a client will be very easy to read, and at other times a client may be very difficult. Sometimes, you will have good days, and at other times you will be off. Don't force things when you are off. It is always best not to do a reading at all than to do a poor or even indifferent one. Though you may not get feedback about positive sessions you have had, you will hear about the poor ones. If you feel you cannot do a satisfactory job, say so. Explain why to the client so that they don't make assumptions about themselves. Honesty is always best, even when you are off.

Never assume: Nothing is more frustrating for a client than not understanding. Don't assume that the client will understand the symbols and images you are impressed with. Neither should you expect the client to interpret the symbol for you. I still often hear readers saying to clients such things as, "I see this large white castle being built. Do you know what this means?" Remember, your subconscious impresses you with the images about the client. You are the only one who can truly interpret it appropriately.

No matter how obvious something seems to you, do not assume the client understands. Ask the client. If there is hesitation or any other indication of no comprehension, re-explain it. Sometimes you may have to say the same thing in three or four ways to get the message across and understood.

Make all explanations simple and basic. Break all of your explanations down as far and as simple as possible. Give examples the client can relate to.

Maintain access to outside referrals and resources: If you work professionally for any length of time, there are individuals who will come to you looking for simple solutions to situations that cannot be resolved quickly or easily. They will be looking for psychic information when it is the last thing they truly need.

As a responsible professional, it is your task to recognize this. You may have strong opinions about what should be done in such things as abuse, for example, but unless you are a trained and qualified abuse counselor or therapist, you have no business messing with this situation. Individuals who come to you with these intense personal problems, do not need or require psychic information. They need therapy and counseling.

What you can do is refer them to appropriate outside sources that are in a much better position to assist them. Use your intuitive abilities to find the best way of directing them to the proper agency or health practitioner. Keep ready a list of addresses and phone numbers of major support groups, social agencies and qualified therapists so that you can make a proper referral.

If the client insists on a psychic reading, use your abilities to help present options that will encourage the individual toward proper therapy. Guiding resolution through appropriate choices and courses of action will enable healing in the most beneficial manner.

Develop objective involvement: This step may be the hardest to accomplish. As a psychic counselor, it is not enough just to provide psychic information. It must be communicated in a responsible and beneficial manner. And whether you wish it or not, there is going to be some involvement.

Involvement, in the sense I am using it, is the ability to communicate your empathy with, your concern for, and your interest in the client—no matter what the problem or life conditions. This means you must accept the clients and treat them as non-judgmentally as possible.

Involvement also means listening to, recognizing and using not just intuitive insights and impressions but everything communicated to you by the client. Pay attention to facial expressions, body motions, voice intonations and other forms of silent language. And keep in mind that sometimes clients just need to be able to express their feelings. Often the simple expression helps them to define their own issues more clearly and initiates healing.

Involvement requires responsibility. You are the outsider looking into another's life, but you are also an outsider who can strongly—for good or bad—affect another's life. Be personable, and let the client feel you are there to work with him or her and help. Don't present yourself as an aloof master. Be objective and warm, and the psychic counseling becomes easier and more productive for both you and the client.

EXERCISES

XXV: Scanning hands

As mentioned earlier, our hands are wonderful tools for feeling. In the palms are minor chakra points. These enable the hands to sense subtle energy or even project it. When applied to detection and of energy in the body and projected for healing purposes, it has been called by many names: the King's touch, etheric healing, therapeutic touch, etc.

Learning to heighten your own hands' sensitivity is actually an easy task. Simply using the methods described earlier in this work will facilitate this process. As your hands become more sensitive, you may wish to use them in healing work. They can be used to assess body energies, and to send energy through them into different parts of the body. For our purposes, we will only be exploring the assessment process. For information on projecting energy through the hands, you may wish to consult two of my earlier works: *How to Heal with Color* and *The Healer's Manual*.

To assess or scan a person is not difficult. Keep in mind, though, that *only* licensed physicians can make diagnoses. Any imbalances you feel should not be labeled, even if you are sure you know what the problem is. Use your hands to detect subtle energy shifts in the body and then describe these shifts. If they must be labeled, allow the individual being scanned to label them. For example, you may feel a coldness in the chest area. It may make you think that there is some congestion, but even this is not for you to say. Describe what you feel to the person. If there is congestion or a cold, the individual usually volunteers that information immediately.

Using the hands to scan the body has most often been associated with spiritual forms of healing. Unfortunately, when you mention that you do spiritual healing, many assume it is healing aligned solely with faith.

Using the hands to scan a person's body is a simple way to determine how a person is or how a person feels in general. This can have both physical, emotional, mental and spiritual connotations. To be truly effective, it will be necessary for both you and the person to be scanned to be relaxed.

Also make sure you understand the process. Practicing with a regular group of individuals is a wonderful way to enhance your abilities and to get immediate feedback so that you can more easily define your impressions. And *never* work with this process, or any form of psychic expression, when tired or ill.

Scanning will help you feel and sense where imbalances are within the energy field of the individual. These imbalances may reflect an actual physical health problem, or they may be symbolic of emotional and mental states. For example, you may sense something different in the areas of the kidneys. It may not indicate an actual kidney dysfunction. Since the kidneys serve to help filter the blood, what you sense with your hands may be symbolic of the individual's lack of discernment and discrimination.

The impressions you pick up with your hands may take any number of expressions. You may detect a change in temperature (warm or cold), a difference in feel (more pressure or even a mushiness). Pay attention to any changes you detect or experience. Pay attention to anything you feel in your own body as your hands pass over the individual you are assessing through the scanning technique. Any changes, any differences will have significance.

1. Always begin by centering yourself. Perform a progressive relaxation or meditation before starting.

2. Rub your hands together briskly for 15 to 20 seconds to stimulate the chakras in them. You may even wish to massage some sandalwood oil or any of the other oils described earlier into the palms to make them more sensitive.

3. Have the individual to be scanned either sitting, standing or reclining in front of you. Assume a position that is most comfortable for you and the individual.

4. Begin with the front side of the individual. Hold your hands out at the top of his/her head about three to six inches from the skin. It does not really matter where you begin, although it often seems more natural to begin at the top of the head and work down to the feet. Slowly draw your hands down the body. Take your time with this. Move slowly over each area. Take at least 15–20 seconds with each part of the body.

5. Pay attention to anything you experience or even imagine that you experience. Take note of them, but do not discuss them at this time. Make a mental note and continue on down the body. Allow your hands to scan the entire front of the body, and then repeat the process with the back of the body. Again make a mental note of any impressions or differences from one area of the body to the next.

6. When you have scanned the entire body, go back and double check any area you were not sure of, or any area you made a mental note about.

7. At this point take a few minutes and discuss with the individual what you experienced and where you felt anything that stood out. Begin by simply describing what you felt. Don't be afraid to ask for feedback or information on possible problems associated with those areas. Examine both the physical possibilities as well as symbolic ones.

It is important to get this confirmation. It will help you in defining your impressions more accurately in the future. It will help you to develop parameters for your own psychic touch. It will help you to develop trust in what you feel. The more practice with this and discussion of it, the better you will get.

8. Some possible guidelines for interpreting what you experience are as follows:

Warm / hot spots: These kinds of impressions can indicate areas either inflamed or overactive. It may indicate chronic problems or a more recent acute problem. It can also indicate an area that is manifesting a physical problem due to some emotional or mental stress. The specific organs or area of the body and its functions will provide clues as to symbolic significance and to possible major issues at play in the individual's life. If warm, these issues are often more aggravating; if cool, they are congestive. Some sample body parts and the issues that can be symbolized by them are:

- Ankles—movement or lack of in life
- Anus—releasing, letting go
- Arms—reaching, holding, embracing
- Bladder (gall)—holding onto the past
- Bladder(urinary)—anger, fear, elimination
- Bones—support (needing and/or lacking)
- Brain—thought process

- Breasts—nurturing & nourishment
- Ears—balance, listening
- Eyes—seeing or refusal to see
- Feet—support or lack of
- Hands—give and take
- Heart—expression of love and emotions
- Hips—balance, support, sexuality
- Intestines—assimilating/eliminating life experiences
- Kidneys—discrimination and discernment
- Liver—criticalness, negative emotions
- Lungs—smothering; expressing life
- Nose—discrimination and discernment
- Pancreas—Sweetness or lack of in life
- Sex Organs—sexuality, creativity
- Stomach—digestion of life's experiences
- Throat—expression, strength of will

Thickness or heaviness in pressure: A thickness in pressure as your hands scan the body may reflect a congestion or a blockage in the normal activity of that particular organ. It may even indicate that the person is not dealing with the issue fully that is symbolized by that part of the body. It can sometimes indicate an area of greater sensitivity, in that the body will sometimes pad an area in the aura with extra energy to cushion and protect it.

Cool / cold Spots: Cool spots encountered during your scanning can easily reflect a blockage in the flow of energy or the functioning of the major organs found in that area or the system of the body with which it is associated. It can reflect poor circulation and movement in some area of the individual's life. Again, by examining the symbolism, you may find the issue of congestion.

XXVI: *Flower clairsentience*

Flower clairsentience is a wonderful form of psychic readings. Flowers are so sensitive, that they easily absorb and are impressed with the energies of the individual handling or possessing them. In this form of psychometry the reader attunes to the impressions left upon the flower. For many beginning psychometrists, working with flower clairsentience can be an effective way of beginning.

There are a variety of ways of performing this form of psychometry. In its most ideal form, the psychometrist does not know whose flower is being read until the end of the session. In group situations the flowers are often tagged and numbered and only after the impressions are given, is the owner identified and the information confirmed or denied. This prevents the psychometrist from unconsciously attuning to the person rather than to the flower. This demonstrates more strongly how objects, especially flowers, will absorb the energies of its owner.

One of the most gifted individuals at performing flower clairsentience is Rev. Bill Landis, a spiritualist medium from England. He often uses flower clairsentience to demonstrate psychic realities, including attunement to spirits. The information he presents is often quite detailed, filled frequently with specific names, initials, events key to the life of the flower's owner. His sessions are always amazing and enjoyable.

There are other variations, and the process is easily adapted for particular situations. I frequently use flower clairsentience for lectures and workshops around Valentine's Day and other romantic holidays. I attune to the flower of the individual and read it to give reflections upon the person's love life, primary lessons and issues in relationships, past problems and even future forecasts in regards to love and romance. It is fun for all concerned, and it does have its benefits.

For many people, flower clairsentience is considered more spiritual than other forms of psychometry. This is because flowers are considered gifts of the Divine.

We will resonate more with some flowers than with others. We will be drawn to certain flowers and their colors and other qualities at certain points in our life. Whether an individual realizes it or not, the flower chosen is going to have strong symbolic significance. The significance will be imprinted upon the flower, and the psychometrists should be able to draw this forth.

Flowers have long been a great source of energy and inspiration. Every aspect of the flower has been used by healers, psychics and metaphysicians. The fragrances, herbal qualities, the colors and the entire imagery of the flowers serve as a tie to and a reflection of specific archetypal forces in nature. We will be drawn to those flowers reflecting the archetypal forces manifesting and affecting our own lives at that time.

Flowers in any form are sources of strong energy vibrations. They influence everything within its area in a very subtle and real manner. They subtly reflect certain qualities or characteristics inherent and active in those people drawn to them. It has to do with an old spiritual principle, "Like attracts like." We are drawn to that which is similar in vibration on some level.

Because of this, every aspect of the flower chosen by an individual to be read will have significance.

All plants that flower are indicative of hidden wisdom. Those flowers we pick out are ones that are more likely to reflect the hidden aspects of your life at this moment, especially those aspects that are most important to you at the time.

The flower's characteristics provide ways of attuning to and interpreting events and issues of the individual's life. For example, as mentioned, I most often perform flower clairsentience in regards to love, romance, and relationships. Every aspect of the flower that an individual has brought to be "read," along with other impressions I pick up from the flower, will have ties to issues and situations involving relationships. This may reflect specific past relationships, past life connections in current relationships and even primary lessons the individual has come to learn in this life about relationships and love in general.

Most people are at least superficially familiar with herbal qualities of flowers and plants. Many flowers, though, have fragrances which can be used to affect certain psychological states as well. These will have significance. Many flowers also have been associated with gods and goddesses, and these can even provide further insight into aspects of the person's life.

If you intend to perform flower clairsentience on a regular basis, it is beneficial to study the symbolism of color, the affects of different fragrances, and even the myths and lore of various flowers.

For most people developing and using their psychic abilities, the most difficult part is getting started. There is a need for something to help them connect more fully with the individual. Beginning with your symbolic interpretations of the flower in general will serve as a bridge that will facilitate your other more subtle impressions in being expressed. It will help you to more fully interpret your impressions and their significance in the life of the flower's owner. At the very least, it starts the flow of information that is significant to the individual. It bridges the conscious mind with your subconscious, making it easier for your own psychometry impressions to surface.

A good example is the lily. Its fragrance is light and airy, and has long been associated with awakening the divine aspects within individuals. Its long stalk is symbolic of the uplifting of the mind. The hanging leaves may reflect a sense of humility, and its whiteness a purity.

If a person came to me for a flower reading with a lily, I would very likely know immediately that this person is seeking a more ideal kind of love and relationship than what has been there in the past. It likely would reflect that the kind of person he or she was looking for had to be very spiritual. It may even reflect a desire to experience a pure love, one that has been untainted. Depending upon what I might also pick up, it may even reflect that he or she doesn't want someone who has been married before or that this person is capable of offering a pure, true love.

Flowers and Their Hidden Significance

Anemone—the higher voice of truth

Angelica—inner light and inspiration

Baby's Breath—modesty, sweet beauty

Begonia—integrated balance

Black-Eyed Susan—emotional insight
and change

Buttercup—healing, understanding,
new directions

Carnation—love of self and life,
physical passion

Chrysanthemum—alchemy, strength-
ened vitality

Daffodil—realization of inner beauty
and higher mind

Daisy—creativity and inner strength
through Nature

Forget-Me-Not—past life memory, ances-
tral lessons and gifts

Gardenia—protection of emotional
well-being

Geranium—renewal of joy in life

Honeysuckle—youthful confidence

Hyacinth—gentleness and expression of
the feminine

Iris—peace, hope for a new birth

Jasmine—self-esteem, transformation

Lily—new birth, purity

Marigold—longevity and fidelity

Orchid—sexuality

Rose—beauty, love, healing of the heart

Snapdragon—protection against unwanted influences

Sunflower—finding and actualizing the inner sun

Tulip—trust and success

Violet—simplicity and modesty

The basic procedures for flower clairsentience are:

1. Have the individual bring a flower. Advise not to allow others to handle or touch the flower once it has been chosen. This ensures that only the owner's imprints are placed upon it.

2. Perform your relaxation exercise and stimulate the chakra centers in the hands.

3. Take the flower from the individual. Softly run your fingers over it. You may wish to place it against the cheek to feel the softness of the petals. Smell it. Note the colors. Take your time with this initial assessment.

4. Pay attention to all that you initially feel and experience. Ask yourself questions throughout. How does the flower feel? Soft? Strong? Stiff? Masculine? Feminine?

5. Note the characteristics of the flower. Is it very fragrant or is it hardly noticeable? What does this say about the individual? What is the significance of the color? Are there any breaks in the flower? Cuts?

The quality and conditions of the flower, its leaves, and the stem may provide indications of an individual's health or the condition of some other aspect of the individual's life. Counting the number provides a trigger, but your own psychometry ability must provide the area of life in which it applies.

Note the numbers found on the flower: number of leaves, buds, thorns, etc. The numbers associated with the flower will always indicate the number of something within an individual's life. For example, the number of leaves or buds may indicate the number of careers, number in the family group or other such information. The number of thorns on the rose may indicate the trouble spots currently or in the past of the individual. If the individual has broken off the thorns, it can reflect the efforts of the individual to eliminate and resolve old sticky problems.

6. Don't be afraid to commit to your impressions. Remember also not to look for feedback along the way. Give out the information. As you continue, the information will elaborate and clarify itself. The time for assessment of your accuracy is at the end. Don't accept a confirmation or settle for it if

it is merely close. It may satisfy the individual, but you want to work constantly toward higher degrees of accuracy and specificity.

XXVII: Locating lost items

Psychometry can be used to attune to a person or an object that has become lost. Although it is not always accurate, it does send a message to the subconscious to bring forth the information—usually when we least expect it.

Individuals that use psychometry to attune to missing or lost individuals usually require some personal article of the individual. I prefer something cloth or an actual article of clothing. This is only effective if it has not been washed recently and has not been handled by a great many other people. If it was worn by the individual just prior to the disappearance, it is even better.

Some psychometrists also work off of photographs of the missing individual. This can also be effective. This is even more so when the photograph is a polaroid. Polaroid pictures capture both the positive and negative ion fields of the individuals, while a photo developed from a negative will only have half of the individual's energy field captured.

This article or photo holds the vibrations of the missing person. There are many subtleties involved in and special to locating lost or missing people. It is not an area that I am comfortable exploring in any great detail in written form, in spite of the potential service it can provide. It is easily misused for personal publicity purposes, money and other reasons. No matter the intention, it can create false hopes, misdirect and even complicate life situations inadvertently.

Our focus will be on something that is more personal to most of us—misplaced or lost items. Occasionally, we all misplace or lose things of importance to us. Some are lost permanently. Others are just misplaced. Some are even stolen.

For anything that is missing, the following form of psychometry can be used to help locate it:

1. You will need a good clear photo of the item, preferably a polaroid. If the missing item is part of a set, such as in the a case of jewelry, it is beneficial to have other pieces of the set to hold and attune to. You may also need a photo or a personal article of the owner of the object, if different from the individual making the request for your psychic search.

If the person seeking the location of an object is not the owner, it is important to get him or her to disclose the reason. It is surprising some of the requests I have had over the years. Some individuals wish to know if certain pieces of jewelry have been buried with its deceased owner. Sometimes individuals want to know if another family member stole the missing object. Sometimes an individual is just sincerely helping a friend. Use a great deal of integrity. Although most individuals will have legitimate reasons, not all will.

2. Having performed your relaxation and preparation, study the photo of the article. Be able to visualize it in your mind's eye while you hold the photo with your eyes closed. Form its image as clearly and as strongly as you can.

Imagine and feel the object. In your mind feel its texture, its shape, its size. Bring it to life within the mind. As you do this, start verbally describing the object and how it feels. Even though the owner knows all of the details of the object, your verbally describing them bridges the conscious mind with the subconscious and helps you to make a link with it.

As you describe the object, you will find other impressions beginning to arise. Give them as immediately as you can. Don't try and make sense out of them. It is important to get the information out. Deciphering it will come later.

The more you do this, the greater the clarity of your impressions. In many ways this vocalizing is like tuning into a radio station so that you can get the channel without any static.

3. Ask yourself questions as you work with the photo. The questions should be phrased in the mind silently, but their answer should be given outwardly so that the question is included. For

example, you may ask yourself silently, "Does another person have possession of this object?" You may be impressed with a "yes" response, so you then audibly speak, "I feel another person does have this object."

The primary reason for this is that it communicates to the subconscious mind that you require complete information and impressions. Vague and abbreviated responses are not suitable. The speaking in complete sentences grounds and crystallizes your impressions. It strengthens the bridge between the subconscious and the conscious for greater psychic information.

Start with general questions and move to the more specific. Then as you phrase and ask your silent questions, the more specific the impressions will come. Some sample general questions are as follows: Is this article lost or stolen? Is it somewhere the individual frequents a lot? Is it at home? Work? Place of recreation? What kind of environment can it be found? Is there something significant about its location? Does someone else have any clues? Are there any colors, images or such that are important to identifying its location? After asking the general questions and speaking your impressions on them, don't hesitate to move to more specific requests. Often specific images and impressions will arise with the asking of a general question. Remember to describe what you get as you get it. Sometimes the process will be slow. Sometimes it will be quick. Be patient with yourself.

4. There are other aids that can be employed to stimulate your intuition through psychometry to locate lost items.

Meditating on the lost object can facilitate an awareness of where it may be found. Most often lost items are simply unconsciously misplaced. Meditation with a brown candle helps to stimulate that level of the subconscious mind that is aware of its location. Brown is the color of St. Anthony who is the patron saint of lost articles.

Holding the hands of the owner is a way of more effectively tuning into the object. The owner has a strong emotional and physical connection to the object. Have the owner focus on the object, visualizing it in his or her possession or in the last place he/she remembers having it. Close your eyes and take the client's hands in your own. Breathe deeply and feel the client's energy. Begin to ask yourself the same questions as above and give forth your impressions.

5. Do not make inadvertent accusations. If you do psychometry searches for lost articles, protect yourself. Lawsuits do occur, and I know of several individuals in the midst of legal battles because of charges of false accusations they made.

Inadvertent and unsubstantiated conclusions and accusations are very damaging to everyone involved. Remember your impressions are only your impressions. There may not be any tangible evidence. Describe your feelings and impressions, but only allow the client to draw conclusions. Keep your personal feelings out of it. You are simply providing a service. Do it as objectively as possible and you will have little or no problems.

There is some metaphysical work that I perform with no fees involved. My healing sessions is one such area. So are situations involving crimes. And there are other areas. For these services, I accept no fees, no donations or anything. If the client feels a need to compensate, I will suggest that they either make a donation to some charity or treat themselves to something they wouldn't otherwise do. My personal philosophy is that I make my money through other areas of the metaphysical realm, and these are my ways of giving back to the universe.

❦

❦ 8 ❧

Precautions
and Protections

For anyone involving themselves in anything of
the psychic realm, practice and training are essential. Without it there will be little control. The
more you develop it, the less likely you will be to
misuse it or have it become intrusive in your life.
Initially, all psychic energy, including psychometry, operates like an artist's energy. It can be very
strong and unbalancing until you learn to turn it
on and off at will.

There can be many blocks to developing your
ability to the fullest, and many of them are subtle.
If you approach its development with the assumption that there really is no logical reason to believe
in it or honor it, your natural abilities will never
blossom. Many people discount what doesn't con-
form to traditional and accepted belief systems
and conventions, and you may find in yourself a
need to root this socialization out of yourself
before its full development can manifest. Of
course, other hindrances are fears, doubts, tension and hurriedness.

Fear and anxiety are great obstacles in the development of any psychic ability, and you must guard against them. Don't allow negative emotions to clutter your mind. Approach development with a cautious optimism. If initially your efforts do not work, avoid self-pity and self-recriminations. Although failure is frustrating, the failure is only this time. Practice and persistence will reward you.

Group development has both advantages and disadvantages. You should keep this in mind before participating with a group. Groups provide a safe, protected, and hopefully, an encouraging climate for your development. They can provide some wonderful assistance in the beginning. Keep in mind though that there may be a time in which you need to move beyond the group, as the group mind can limit the growth of the individual. You must also learn to use your ability outside of the group environment. If you don't, you may find your abilities more intermittent and less reliable than in the group environment.

Sometimes it is best not to let others know of your development. Some people may be supportive, but others will not. They will be skeptical and demand proof of your ability. Nothing pleases these people more than providing tests that you cannot fully pass. Oftentimes, failures in such situations are the result of anxiety over performing successfully for these individuals. Such situations serve to deteriorate your own self-confidence.

Keep in mind that psychometry is a natural ability for everyone. It is more easily developed than other forms of psychism, but as with them all, it needs to be encouraged and disciplined.

Don't be too eager to step out and demonstrate your ability. Until you develop it fully, it is easy to exhaust yourself. Wanting to demonstrate also reflects that there are ego issues that you need to deal with. Be very careful of walking around trying to be tuned in all the time.

This is a problem for many old-time mediums and psychics. They stay tuned into everyone and everything they encounter, afraid to shut it down. They often fear that they will not be able to turn it on again. This is a fallacy and extremely unhealthy. We can learn to turn it on and off at will and to whatever degree we desire.

You may have experienced or seen mediums and psychics who look as if they have been run through a wringer. They look tired and ill. Their health is often poor. In such cases, it should make you question their abilities. The psychic information must be translated through the medium of the body. If the body is out of balance, it is very likely that the information will be also.

People who learn to truly develop and control their intuitive faculties will be strong and vibrant.

No matter what age they are, there will be a vitality about them that is eternal. These individuals have gained positive control over their faculties. They do not allow it to function without their conscious permission (except in exceptional cases), and they are able to use it to some degree under all circumstances and conditions. These are the psychics who never use it without regard for limits of time, moral obligations and their own physical endurance.

There is great responsibility for anyone developing and using their psychic abilities, especially professionally and publicly. You must control your emotional reactions to what you receive. If impressed with negative, you must develop an ability to state it in a tactful way, a way that enables the individual to see options and alternatives.

The question of fate versus free will is one that will arise time and again. Just because you have received an impression does not mean that the events surrounding it can't be changed. The changing of it may be difficult, and may simply involve helping an individual change his or her perception of the events about to unfold. The individual must know that there is truly nothing which can't be altered to some degree. There are always choices. There are always options.

Discretion is of utmost importance. I still frequently hear psychics discussing clients among themselves. An individual who comes to a psychic for any reason, should expect client confidentiality. Never discuss with others information that you received psychically about a client. I have known many psychics who use their abilities to feed their need for gossip. It is disrespectful, unethical and even cruel.

Psychometry can be developed and used by anyone. Its development does not require any higher moral development than does developing greater strength. Nor does having this ability reflect a higher degree of spiritual development any more than having great strength would.

Maintaining Balance in Your Development

The key ingredients to helping yourself stay balanced and protected in your development are simple—proper diet, exercise, and fresh air. You do not have to become a vegetarian or live an ascetic life. Moderation in all things is enough. Keep in mind, though, that drugs, alcohol, tobacco, stress, and trauma will interfere with your abilities.

Three considerations are most effective in maintaining balance as you awaken to your developing faculties:

Increase your water intake: Most people do not drink enough water anyway, but this is especially important for those individuals developing their psychic abilities. When we begin to work with higher psychic energies we need to increase water. Water is an excellent conductor of energy. It facilitates attunement without becoming short circuited by its higher intensity. Whenever I am doing extensive psychic work or just lecturing and teaching, I make sure I drink what seems to many an excessive amount of water, but it is beneficial for overall attunement.

Fast periodically: It enables the body to rest. We expend more energy through digestion than through any other bodily function. When the body gets periodic breaks from digestion, it can more easily stimulate and focus energies into other forms of expression. This in turn helps us to be more cognizant of our intuitive faculties.

Fasting also helps eliminate impurities from our systems that can inhibit our higher and more subtle perceptions. It becomes easier to discern and discriminate about our psychic impressions and to utilize them more effectively.

Meditate: Traditionally there have been two primary methods for drawing out power: meditative and ceremonial. We will concentrate on meditation. Meditative techniques are simpler and are varied. These include symbology, visualization, creative imagination, pathworking, chanting and mantras, yantras, etc. For any meditational method to work to its fullest capacity, we must concentrate upon our development and the spiritual unfoldment that will come of it. In this way, we keep ourselves grounded, and we increase our awareness of the universe and our connection to it and all that exists within it.

Much has been written about meditation and its various practices. In fact, there are as many methods of meditation as there are people. As to which method or combination of methods is best for you, no one can truly answer that but you. Work with various methods. Experiment, and find which works best for you.

When we close our eyes and withdraw our senses from the outer world around us, we enter another realm of life entirely. It is more fleeting and more fluid than our physical world. It also operates according to what can seem to be strange laws. As different as it may seem, it is as real as our world in the physical. It has the power to reflect and touch our lives in ways we are still only beginning to comprehend. It is a world where we can dream, ponder the future, rediscover the past and unveil mysteries and questions that surround us.

Through meditation, we begin to awaken and utilize our inner potentials. We activate inner energies, awaken our intuitive faculties and integrate our bodies, minds and spirits for greater growth. Through meditation we gain a new perspective on our life experiences and we can begin to use greater knowledge to affect both current and future life experiences.

Through meditation, we gain control over our lives, and we begin to understand how energy works in, through and around us. Through meditation we touch that part of the divine that resides within each of us—that hidden source of light, protection, creativity and intuition.

EXERCISES

XXVIII: *Preparing to meditate*

Meditation triggers higher forms of inspiration and intuition. It begins to unveil the microcosm working within our day to day lives. It helps give us an understanding of the conditions of our lives and the spiritual laws that govern it.

Most metaphysicians and occultists believe that our real psychic and spiritual powers lie within the inner realms, which are hinted to us through dreams. Various methods of meditation make it possible to bring through to the conscious mind and conscious expression the wealth of our inner resources.

The key to learning to empower your life through meditation is to set up conditions that create a mental shift to a new way of processing information—an altered state of consciousness. Through meditation, we learn to delve into parts of the mind too often obscured by the endless details of daily life. We begin to see underlying patterns, and we develop the ability to more fully access greater potential and release it into our waking consciousness.

To achieve these results, we need to shift our awareness and then maintain it for the time and purpose necessary. Controlled meditation is a learned skill. As with all learned skills, it requires practice and increasing reinforcement. The first steps are most crucial. If the preliminaries to meditation are followed, it won't matter which particular form you then choose to use. Any will be effective. The key is relaxation!

1. Find a comfortable space. It can be sitting upright or lying down. Often sitting is recommended as in the prone position, it is easy to fall asleep.

2. Make sure you will not be disturbed. This is your sacred time, a time for your own personal exploration. Remove the phone from the hook and eliminate as many auditory distractions as possible.

3. Begin to perform deep breathing. Inhale for a count of four, hold for a count of eight to 10, and then exhale for a count of four. Keep the breaths slow and regular.

4. Now perform a slow progressive relaxation. Take your time with this. Don't hurry. The longer you take, the more relaxed you will become. The more relaxed you are, the easier it is to manifest your inner potentials.

5. At some point in the relaxation, you will encounter resistance. The mind will start to wander. You will start thinking about the day's activities, etc. Do not get upset over this. It is a positive sign!

This reflects that you have accessed the subconscious mind, which is where you want to be. The resistance is the subconscious resisting your direction. If you've never meditated, the subconscious is not used to being controlled and directed. It is not disciplined. It tries to run wherever it wishes—usually where you do not want it to go.

When this occurs, simply return your focus to your progressive relaxation. You may have to do this repeatedly, but by doing so you are training the subconscious to follow your conscious dictates rather than its own. You are teaching it to do what you will it to.

6. Once you are relaxed, focus or concentrate upon an image or an idea. In our case, you may want to focus on the image of your hands being more psychically sensitive. Visualize as much about this as possible. Allow images and scenarios to run through the mind in which you see yourself touching and holding people and things and "reading" them very accurately. Visualize all that you are able to do with this ability. Visualize it as if it is already active and strong within you. There is no future; there is no past. To the subconscious mind, there is only an eternal present moment. Visualize, imagine, taste, touch, smell and hear everything that you are able to do with this ability. Make it as concrete in your mind as possible. Remember that the only language that the subconscious mind knows is symbology. Thus the stronger your images, the stronger you communicate your demands to the subconscious so that you inner abilities awaken and unfold.

7. Enjoy the reverie. As you meditate, allow the images and thoughts surrounding the focus to pass by. Note them, and allow them to simply flow. They will be remembered, and they will register. Do not try to analyze them. Let your mind enjoy the reverie.

8. Allow yourself to gently return to a conscious awareness. Know that as you do, your abilities return with you stronger and more vibrant than ever, increasing with each passing minute.

9. Take a deep breath and feel yourself grounded and balanced in your body and mind. You may want to have some closing gesture as a signal to help ground you after this altered state. Eating something light (such as crackers) will help keep you grounded.

10. Initially, your meditations will be longer, but as you develop your ability to relax and shift awareness, it will not take as long. Meditations should rarely be longer than a half-hour to 45 minutes. If they are consistently so, you may be using them as a form of escapism. What will take the longest in the beginning is the relaxing. After it is mastered, your creative meditations can be easily accomplished within 10 minutes or even less.

During your meditation, your altered state of consciousness, there will be experienced some phenomena. These may include some or all of the following:

- Distortion of time-flashes of light.
- Body movements: heaviness or lightness.
- Flashes of color-sensation of falling asleep.
- Sounds—growing/shrinking feelings.
- Images—pulling/stretching feelings.

❦ 9 ❧

Personal Empowerment

Positive psychism requires control of your senses and faculties. It demands the ability to turn them on and off at will. It should always serve and be beneficial to the individual, and should only be used consciously at the right time, in the right way and in the right proportion to the person. If you are not sure of your abilities, then you should not be demonstrating them until you are. We don't have to be perfect in all of this, but we should be working toward some higher degree of perfection.

Proper development of any of your intuitive faculties has many beneficial effects:

- Better health.
- Less stress.
- Aids in decisions.
- More control over your life.
- Enhances your creativity.
- Awakens even greater potentials.
- Energizes you while it relaxes you.
- Greater perspective on life and all its situations.

- Past life information.
- Spiritual development.
- Greater balance.
- Greater control of all the energies encountered in life.
- Greater discernment and discrimination.
- Opportunity to assist others.
- Greater recognition and realization of higher forces operating within our lives.

True psychism and its many benefits will never be fully developed and experienced if you begin working with the public too soon. Initially, the energy stimulated through development serves to change your own individual frequency so that you are more able to handle higher intensities. If you step too quickly out into the public, you will dissipate the energy that otherwise would have enabled you to transmute your own personal energies into a higher, more dynamic and spiritual vibration.

As the psychometrist, you are the mediator and interpreter for your client. You have the responsibility to act consciously for the individual. Always know what the nature of the psychic message is and how to convey it so as not to overly influence or intrude upon the individual's free will.

You are also always free to refuse anything that does not feel right. If you are not comfortable with a situation or an individual, you do not have to work with it. Just because you have developed your ability and put yourself out to the public, does not mean you have to be open to serve anyone and everyone. You have the right to use your own discretion and discrimination. Don't make yourself a martyr. It does a great disservice to you and to your client.

Keep your messages and impressions in the nature of inspiration and related to the plane of service. You dishonor your ability and yourself through using it to uncover gossip and such. In this way, it will always energize you and those you touch. It will increase your creativity, vitality and joy. As a result, you will find yourself increasingly magnetic, drawing more and more people to you.

At a certain point in your development, you will be able to understand all that you intuitively receive as you receive it. The information will come in wholes and in the interest of the individual with whom you are working. You will become a power house of psychic energy which encourages, heals, leads and protects others.

You will find that you do not have to make self-claims. Your field of service will gradually but continually expand. You will have increasing control on your urges, drives and your ability to transmute them into higher forms of expression. You will work increasingly with the laws of privacy and responsibility.

As you develop your higher faculties through learning such techniques as psychometry, you will discover that you increasingly know about others around you. You will find that you have increasing discrimination so as not to reveal what could be misused or misunderstood. You will find your power to influence people for good or bad increasing and demanding greater discernment in its application.

You will learn to see and not reveal what you see. You will touch others with healing energies while within their presence without having to consciously work to heal them. Others will become so stimulated by your own light and energy that they will be able to see and understand what they previously had not seen or understood without you having to directly make revelations to them.

As you develop your own innate abilities, you will enlighten, heal and help free those you touch. You will stimulate others to a new continuity of consciousness. With your increasing ability to recognize and know karma and to cooperate with the laws of the universe, you will touch others in a way that gives greater meaning to their lives and your own.

There has always been a great deal of mystery surrounding the human essence, and we may never truly know all that it is capable of. Methods though for exploring our many possibilities have been around since more ancient times. All of these methods require that we be willing to commit time, energy and patience in their discovery. For many people, the so-called psychic realm still assumes a supernatural caricature, but in every person the qualities essential for accelerating our growth are innate. The potential to accelerate and awaken our own divine characteristics lie within reach of each one of us without exception.

In unfolding this potential, we are often our own worst enemies. We either won't or can't make the most of our opportunities. We do not put forth the time and energy, becoming too impatient for the imagined rewards of the development. We may even resort to quick methods that ultimately create tremendously damaging difficulties down the road for us. Often times, we may halt because the process is too great or demands too much effort. There is no true shortcut though.

As we develop any one of our capabilities, it becomes easier to develop and manifest them all. Manifesting a higher destiny requires a higher search for knowledge while striving to fulfill the obligations of life. It demands a fully conscious union with the creative, super sensible realms.

This is not fulfilled through demonstrations of psychic abilities. Psychic power in itself simply hints at realms and possibilities that are even more wondrous than what we have ever imagined.

As we develop any inner potential we empower our lives and our souls. Instead of seeing our path as one that leads into some blinding light into which all of our troubles are dissolved, we begin to realize the well of truth and light that lies within us. As we empower ourselves, we cease looking for some light to shine down upon us, and we begin looking for the light within to shine out from us!

❦ Bibliography ❦

Andrews, Ted. *How To See and Read the Aura.* Llewellyn Publications; St. Paul, 1991.

Brennan, Barbara Ann. *Hands of Light.* Bantam Books, New York, 1988.

Butler, W. E. *How to Read the Aura, Practice Psychometry, Telepathy and Clairvoyance.* Warner Destiny Books; New York, 1978.

Cosimano, Charles. *Psionics 101.* Llewellyn Publications, St. Paul, 1987.

De A'morelli, Richard. *ESP Party Games.* Major Books, Chatsworth, California, 1976.

Denning, Melita and Phillips, Osborne. *Development of Psychic Power.* Llewellyn Publications, St. Paul, 1988.

Evans, W.H. *How To Be A Medium.* Lumen Press; St, Louis.

Holzer, Hans. *ESP and You.* Ace Books, New York, 1966.

_____. *Truth About ESP.* Manor Books, New York, 1974.

Manning, Al G. *Helping Yourself with ESP.* Parker Publication, New York, 1966.

Merrill, Joseph. *Mediumship.* National Spiritualist Association, New York, 1971.

Vishita, Swami. *Genuine Mediumship and the Invisible Powers.* Yogi Publication Society, Chicago, 1919.

Weston, Victoria. *Selecting Your Psychic.* Oscar-Dey Publishing; Atlanta, 1988.

Wilber, Ken, Ed. *The Holographic Paradigm.* New Science Library, Boulder, 1982.

❦

On the following pages you will find listed, with their current prices, some of the books now available on related subjects. Your book dealer stocks most of these and will stock new titles in the Llewellyn series as they become available. We urge your patronage.

TO GET A FREE CATALOG

To obtain our full catalog, you are invited to write (see address below) for our bi-monthly news magazine/catalog, *Llewellyn's New Worlds of Mind and Spirit*. A sample copy is free, and it will continue coming to you at no cost as long as you are an active mail customer. Or you may subscribe for just $10 in the United States and Canada ($20 overseas, first class mail). Many bookstores also have *New Worlds* available to their customers. Ask for it.

TO ORDER BOOKS AND TAPES

If your book store does not carry the titles described on the following pages, you may order them directly from Llewellyn by sending the full price in U.S. funds, plus postage and handling (see below).

Credit card orders: VISA, MasterCard, American Express are accepted. Call us toll-free within the United States and Canada at 1-800-THE-MOON.

Postage and Handling: Include $4 postage and handling for orders $15 and under; $5 for orders *over* $15. There are no postage and handling charges for orders over $100. Postage and handling rates are subject to change. We ship UPS whenever possible within the continental United States; delivery is guaranteed. Please provide your street address as UPS does not deliver to P.O. boxes. Orders shipped to Alaska, Hawaii, Canada, Mexico and Puerto Rico will be sent via first class mail. Allow 4-6 weeks for delivery. **International orders:** Airmail – add retail price of each book and $5 for each non-book item (audiotapes, etc.); Surface mail – add $1 per item.

Minnesota residents add 7% sales tax.
Llewellyn Worldwide
P.O. Box 64383-025, St. Paul, MN 55164-0383, U.S.A.
For customer service, call (612) 291-1970.
Prices subject to change without notice.

THE HEALER'S MANUAL
A Beginner's Guide to Vibrational Therapies
Ted Andrews

Did you know that a certain Mozart symphony can ease digestion problems ... that swelling often indicates being stuck in outworn patterns ... that breathing pink is good for skin conditions and loneliness? Most dis-ease stems from a metaphysical base. While we are constantly being exposed to viruses and bacteria, it is our unbalanced or blocked emotions, attitudes and thoughts that deplete our natural physical energies and make us more susceptible to "catching a cold" or manifesting some other physical problem.

Healing, as approached in *The Healer's Manual*, involves locating and removing energy blockages wherever they occur—physical or otherwise. This book is an easy guide to simple vibrational healing therapies that anyone can learn to apply to restore homeostasis to their body's energy system. By employing sound, color, fragrance, etheric touch and flower/gem elixers, you can participate actively within the healing of your body and the opening of higher perceptions. You will discover that you can heal more aspects of your life than you ever thought possible.

0-87542-007-9, 256 pgs., 6 x 9, illus., softcover $12.95

HOW TO HEAL WITH COLOR
by Ted Andrews
Now, for perhaps the first time, color therapy is placed within the grasp of the average individual. Anyone can learn to facilitate and accelerate the healing process on all levels with the simple color therapies in *How to Heal with Color*.

Color serves as a vibrational remedy that interacts with the human energy system to stabilize physical, emotional, mental and spiritual conditions. When there is balance, we can more effectively rid ourselves of toxins, negativities and patterns that hinder our life processes.

This book provides color application guidelines that are beneficial for over 50 physical conditions and a wide variety of emotional and mental conditions. Receive simple and tangible instructions for performing "muscle testing" on yourself and others to find the most beneficial colors. Learn how to apply color therapy through touch, projection, breathing, cloth, water and candles. Learn how to use the little known but powerful color-healing system of the mystical Qabala to balance and open the psychic centers. Plus, discover simple techniques for performing long distance healings on others.
0-87542-005-2, 240 pgs., mass market, illus. $4.99

HOW TO SEE AND READ THE AURA
by Ted Andrews

Everyone has an aura—the three-dimensional, shape-and-color-changing energy field that surrounds all matter. And anyone can learn to see and experience the aura more effectively. There is nothing magical about the process. It simply involves a little understanding, time, practice and perseverance.

Do some people make you feel drained? Do you find some rooms more comfortable and enjoyable to be in? Have you ever been able to sense the presence of other people before you actually heard or saw them? If so, you have experienced another person's aura. In this practical, easy-to-read manual, you receive a variety of exercises to practice alone and with partners to build your skills in aura reading and interpretation. Also, you will learn to balance your aura each day to keep it vibrant and strong so others cannot drain your vital force.

Learning to see the aura not only breaks down old barriers—it also increases sensitivity. As we develop the ability to see and feel the more subtle aspects of life, our intuition unfolds and increases, and the childlike joy and wonder of life returns.

0-87542-013-3, 160 pgs., mass market, illus. $3.95

HOW TO MEET & WORK WITH SPIRIT GUIDES
by Ted Andrews

We often experience spirit contact in our lives but fail to recognize it for what it is. Now you can learn to access and attune to beings such as guardian angels, nature spirits and elementals, spirit totems, archangels, gods and goddesses— as well as family and friends after their physical death.

Contact with higher soul energies strengthens the will and enlightens the mind. Through a series of simple exercises, you can safely and gradually increase your awareness of spirits and your ability to identify them. You will learn to develop an intentional and directed contact with any number of spirit beings. Discover meditations to open up your subconscious. Learn which acupressure points effectively stimulate your intuitive faculties. Find out how to form a group for spirit work, use crystal balls, perform automatic writing, attune your aura for spirit contact, use sigils to contact the great archangels and much more! Read *How to Meet and Work with Spirit Guides* and take your first steps through the corridors of life beyond the physical.

0–87542–008–7, 192 pgs., mass market, illus. $4.99